How *to* Avoid Making *a* Fool *of* Yourself

An Introduction to General Semantics

R. Wayne Pace

INSTITUTE OF GENERAL SEMANTICS

OTHER TITLES INCLUDED IN
The New Non-Aristotelian Library Series
Corey Anton, Series Editor

Korzybski, Alfred (2010). *Selections from Science and Sanity.* (2nd Ed.). Edited by Lance Strate, with a Foreword by Bruce I. Kodish. Fort Worth, TX: Institute of General Semantics.

Strate, Lance (2011). *On the Binding Biases of Time and Other Essays on General Semantics and Media Ecology.* Fort Worth, TX: Institute of General Semantics.

Anton, Corey (2011). *Communication Uncovered: General Semantics and Media Ecology.* Fort Worth, TX: Institute of General Semantics.

Levinson, Martin H. (2012). *More Sensible Thinking.* New York, NY: Institute of General Semantics.

Anton, Corey & Strate, Lance (2012). *Korzybski and...* (Eds.) New York, NY: Institute of General Semantics.

Levinson, Martin H. (2014). *Continuing Education Teaching Guide to General Semantics.* New York, NY: Institute of General Semantics.

Berger, Eva & Berger, Isaac. (2014). *The Communication Panacea: Pediatrics and General Semantics.* New York, NY: Institute of General Semantics.

Contents

Preface

In this book, you're going to be learning a great deal about language and behavior, especially about how we speak and write and behave. I suspect that we need to explain why we take such an emphasis. The following paragraphs address questions related to such proclivities.

Why write about writing, speaking, and behaving?

The most common, consistent, pervasive, perplexing, dull, entertaining, and positively entrancing feature of living as a human being in this world concerns **the effect that language use has** on how we **think about, perceive, and describe** people, objects, and happenings, and how we **respond** to how we think, perceive, and describe people, objects, and happenings. Our innate agency allows us to make up statements, descriptions, and predictions about the world in which we live and the inhabitants living therein that both meet and fail the tests of reliability, validity, authenticity, veracity, and truthfulness.

What do we mean by "Facts" and "Truth"?

These terms--facts and truth—tend to appear throughout this book in reference, primarily, to the end result of our perceptions of things in the world and how we talk about them. What does it mean to "get a fact" or utter a "truth"? We'd like to offer a definition of both terms that may help us to recognize facts when we see them and to make as many accurate and useful and truthful statements as possible. Most of us dislike people who fail to recognize facts and who habitually utter untruthful statements. If you have those kinds of failings, people may not like you either.

Facts versus Fantasies. We'd like to use the term, *fact,* to refer to something that actually exists; statements about things that don't exist, we shall call, "fantasy." We shall call statements that refer to things that exist, "Statements of Fact." To us a *fact* exits at the nonverbal level of experience. Words and facts represent quite different things. You can't "say" a fact but you can make statements about a fact. If you make a "statement of fact," you attempt to say something about a fact, then you have an obligation to show the fact to which the statement refers; otherwise, we'll refer to such statements as "inferences."

Inferences versus Facts. An inference represents a statement about a so-called fact that you have difficulties pointing to or verifying, so you have to make a guess about whether a person, object, or event actually exists or existed or did something. When you doubt whether a fact exists, ask the person making the statement to show you the fact in question. A lot of words and statements do not refer to the existence of things or you just cannot find them in reality. For example, you can't show another person "gravity," but you can show them something falling. You just infer that gravity had something to do with the falling rock.

Truths versus Falsehoods. We'd like to use the term, *truth,* to refer only to **"statements that confirm or verify the real things, events, and facts that exist in the world."** Thus, we say that the word fact refers or points to a nonverbal thing that exists, and truth consists of **statements that actually verify that nonverbal things exist.** We'll call **any statement** that confirms any reality—from the smallest physical particle to the largest physical phenomenon to even an actual spiritual experience, if they confirm the actuality of something—a statement of *Truth.* You may have a difficult time distinguishing between a statement of fact and a statement of truth, since they tend to refer to the same process.

How to Determine the Truth of a Statement

None of the above, however, addresses the issue of HOW one determines a "fact" or "a truth." We feel that one may confirm a statement about a "fact" more readily than the "truth" of a statement. However, we can say that a person may verify a "fact" by simply pointing to an actual nonverbal person, object, or event without talking about it. To verify a "truth," one must provide some form of evidence that the statement actually refers to some real thing and that the real thing actually exists. For us to call something a "truth," the person uttering the statement must provide some evidence that the statement refers to something that actuality exists. Otherwise, the statement must be called a "prediction" or a statement of "great confidence." We may not know the extent to which a statement of truth can be verified, but we can accept the idea that you feel you have a *high level of confidence in the statement.* We'll assume that such statements may or may not refer to some real thing, but you assert that they do.

False and Untrue Statements

From almost the beginning of time, our intelligence, good will, graciousness, and ability to challenge, question, doubt, and affirm people's use of language for both good and evil has allowed us to recognize and confront those who consciously, deliberately, intentionally, willfully, and purposefully misrepresent the people, objects, and events in the world. However, we often appear to lack the ability to detect accidental, unintended, inadvertent, unpremeditated, uncalculated, involuntary, unwitting, and unconscious inaccuracies in language use. And, if detected, we tend to brush over and unequivocally forgive, and find them unabashedly entertaining.

We tend to disregard the agonizing consequences on ourselves and on others of persistent, unyielding, tenacious, indefatigable, dogged, and stubborn uses of inaccurate, untenable, flawed, faulty, specious, thoughtless, injudicious, and imprudent uses of our language. We often relish, enjoy, find delight in, appreciate, and respond with gusto to gross inaccuracies, distortions, imprecisions, inexactness, looseness, exaggerations, hyperboles, and downright fallaciousness. Most humor involves overstatement, understatement, and untruthful utterances. Popular songs use hyperbole, excess, distortion, embellishment, and caricature in their lyrics.

False statements assert something that does not exist. For example, if you claim that New York City is located in New Mexico, we say that you made a false statement because we can verify the location of NYC. If you say, I did not hit a specific person, but you actually did hit the person, we say that you made a false statement.

> *Real tough problems*
> *Don't faze me a bit;*
> *If at first I don't succeed,*
> *I quit.*

Unconditional Statements as Falsehoods

I'd lie for you, and that's the truth!

Few things cloud our thinking about other people as much as uttering unconditional statements. An unconditional statement asserts that something will occur without any reservations or conditions. In other words, unconditional statements claim that something will be achieved regardless of what may happen to the contrary. Unconditional statements are generally offered with great confidence.

The most effective unconditional statements begin with the words "I am . . . ," "I can . . . ," or "I will . . . ." The most accomplished users of the unconditional promise generally switch from the first person singular to the use of plural words, such as "We are. . . ," "We can. . . ," or "We will. . .," The unconditional statement asserts that something is true **that is not quite yet true**. It promises something that is wonderfully desirable, **but that is not yet available.** Hearers want the claims to be true and they often try to make them come true, but usually without avail.

Unconditional statements get their strength from the social phenomenon called *veridicality* or the assumption that the person uttering the statement is truthful, and that he or she is decent, pleasant, and trustworthy. This is why new coaches, managers, and politicians, use unconditional statements; it allows them to begin with a positive bias on their behalf. Such statements, however, radiate dishonesty, crookedness, and deceit. Unconditional statements promise outcomes that cannot be achieved. They represent the grossest of overgeneralizations that have little likelihood of being carried out.

Politicians are usually quite skilled at articulating unconditional statements. Some examples include extending health care to everyone at a lower cost, providing more education for young people, creating a new economy, allowing more stem cell research, expanding oil production, presenting a frugal national budget to Congress, and reducing the national debt.

In a world of constant and tumultuous, change, the promises projected by unconditional statements are the most difficult to keep. Most unconditional promises are delayed for long periods of time, and, since they are difficult to fulfill, most fail.

Although unconditional statements appear to exude a positive atmosphere, they are some of the most deadly deceptions perpetuated on people because they are based on the assumption that all things are possible, which is just not the case (see, Smith, 1976, *How to Cure Yourself of Positive Thinking*).

Another issue has to do with what someone means when they make a statement. Let's examine this issue in a little more depth.

Types of Meanings

We usually talk about two different types of meanings, ***denotative and connotative.*** ***Denotative*** meanings refer to or verbally point to an object, person, or happening. We usually call the things to which words point denotatively, *referents.* Nouns and verbs point to referents of different types—nouns to people and objects and verbs to ways of acting.

Connotative meanings refer to affective or emotional tones attached to words and develop out of our own personal experiences; ultimately, all connotations represent private and personal meanings. Scientists try, more or less successfully, to develop names and descriptions of their products that avoid connotative meanings (Weaver and Strausbaugh, 1964, pp. 28-29).

Metaphors and Connotative Meaning

Metaphors reveal the idea of connotative meanings most clearly. When we talk about one thing as if it existed as something else, we create metaphors. Margaret Schlauch's (1955) stimulating book about language explains the everyday use of metaphors, which she calls "the extension of words to include new referents somehow resembling the original ones." She cites examples involving parts of the body, such as "the lip of a cup," or the "teeth of a saw," or "the hands of a clock."

She also lists animal's members, such as "goose-neck lamps," and "rats of hair," and "beak of a vessel," and "monkey wrench." Plants and tools names often evolve into metaphors, such as "stem of a glass," or "root of a tooth'" or "fork in a road," or "vocal cords," or "bridge of the nose," or the "ear drum."

What, for example, do these frivolous tips for fitness mean? "Walk on eggs, throw a fit, stretch the truth, sweat bullets, skate on thin ice, jump to conclusions, pass the buck, bend over backwards, open a can of worms, count eggs before they hatch, hit the nail on the head, drag your heels, and make mountains out of molehills." Such statements seem clever, but they raise serious questions about the accuracy, factualness, and truthfulness of such utterances.

The construction of metaphors makes the denotative meaning of the words nonsensical. For example, the metaphor of a rose and its color represents a nonsensical expression; statements such as "the rose is red" tend to make the object, Rose, the same as the word red, which cannot be done. The word Red and the object Rose exist in totally different ways and cannot exist as one thing. Statements such as, "He is a tiger," makes the denotative meaning nonsensical, although connotatively, the phrase may have some meaning for select individuals.

We wrote this book to shed some light on the chilling and often devastating outcomes of both serious and shallow language patterns. We think that some analyses of foundational explanations may provide some support for our suggested changes. We also feel that connecting language habits with their detrimental effects may lend some credibility to our recommendations.

Why write a book without using the verb TO BE?

For the most part, this book avoids most uses of the verb "to be." The verb to be represents one of the most frequently occurring language disorders that come from teachings in elementary schools and other places that urge and even insist that we use the passive verb "to be," and its rampant variations. The *Harbrace College Handbook* (1977) of the English language explains that verbs represent "a part of speech denoting action, occurrence, or existence (state of being). Inflections indicate tense and sometimes person and number and the mood of a verb. Transitive verbs have voice. A verb with a direct object is in the *active* voice. When the direct object is converted into a subject . . . , the verb is in the *passive* voice. A passive verb is always a verb phrase consisting of a form of the verb *be* or sometimes *get* followed by a past participle" (p. 447). Examples of the active voice include, Priscilla hired John, Ed studies language, and Lacy and Merle live on the same street; and John was chosen by Priscilla, English is a language, and Merle was fired, illustrate the passive voice.

An important issue, as far as our concerns go, states that "because of lost inflections, modern English depends heavily on word order to convey meaning." E-Prime English represents a fundamental re-ordering of words and reflects a major adjustment in the meaning of utterances. Thus, please observe carefully how we restructure sentences when we omit the verb "to be." We think you'll appreciate the impact of this re-ordering of sentences and may even join us in perpetuating such changes in your own language patterns.

Why focus on *borderline* maladjustments?

As we point out in the body of the book, we want to deter disorders and maladjustment, rather than to pursue an after-the-fact, pathological, clinical healing process. We would like to assist you in catching yourself before serious damage occurs. We like the idea of counteracting tendencies toward maladjustment before they emerge as major disorders of evaluation and meaning. The idea of focusing on potential or borderline difficulties appealed to us, so we took that line and trust that you may also appreciate such an approach.

Who contributed the most in helping you write this book?

I said, "Gae, my spouse, made the single most significant contribution to me by providing an environment that allowed me to ponder the questions and answers associated with this book."

R. Wayne Pace
St. George, Utah

> *At a bankers' dinner the other evening,*
> *a banker read a bad poem that he wrote,*
> *and nothing was done about it.*
> *But let a poet write a bad check!*

Pre-Reading Assessment

You may skip this part of the book, but many people like to discover what they don't know about a topic before they plunge into the heart of it. Just in case you happen to have the urge to find out what you know about language and its effect on behavior before you read this book, we've provided an assessment involving a number of statements that we feel represent true or false assertions. Just circle your choice and when you finish, turn to Appendix A and check the key for our choices.

Instructions: Read each statement and decide whether you consider it True or False. Circle T or F to indicate your choice.

1. The assumptions of probability fit the structure of reality better than assumptions of certainty.   T   F

2. An inferential statement represents what a person observes.   T   F

3. Non-allness oriented people think they know it all.   T   F

4. Meanings exist in words.   T   F

5. Verbal and Nonverbal realities consist of the same elements.   T   F

6. A multivalued orientation makes third alternatives difficult to achieve.   T   F

7. A misevaluation fails to fit the facts.   T   F

8. We may make both statements of fact and statements of inference after an observation.   T   F

9. A verbal reaction occurs when you pinch your finger.   T   F

10. Abstracting involves selecting some characteristics and eliminating others.   T   F

11. Vague, abstract and ambiguous words fit the category of low order abstractions.   T   F

12. Either-or assertions with no middle ground represent the contrary type.   T   F

13. We can abstract everything in some situations.   T   F

14. More misunderstandings tend to occur when we use high-order abstractions.   T   F

15. One can make an unlimited number of inferential statements about people.   T F

16. People who think they know it all have a high consciousness of abstracting.   T F

17. People's past experience represents an important determinant in the meanings of words.   T F

18. In talking with others, we tend to use more contrary words than contradictory ones.   T F

19. Being conscious of abstracting and the use of "etc" represent two ways of reducing allness statements.   T F

20. The term "organism" represents a higher order of abstraction than the word "man."   T F

21. If we study something long enough, we can know all about it.   T F

22. In some situations, "silence" may indicate hostility.   T F

23. Statements appearing in a newspaper should represent statements of a fact to its readers.   T F

24. The unconscious assumption that meanings reside in people leads to most misunderstandings.   T F

25. Arguing at the extreme poles of an issue allows differences to reduce.   T F

26. If a word that you don't know the meaning of comes up in conversation, go to a dictionary and avoid complicating the situation by asking the person what it means.   T F

27. Unhappiness usually results from our own assumptions and expectations rather than from what other people do.   T F

28. Contradictories and contraries tend to represent the same language pattern.   T F

29. The "container" assumption says that people hold the meanings of words.   T F

30. Using bipolar terms we give situations multivalued orientations.   T F

31. To lessen misunderstanding, use more symbol reactions.   T F

32. To say, "I don't know" admits to your own ignorance, which represents a bad trait in an intelligent person.   T F

33. A sign of mature behavior occurs when you use inferences as if they consisted of factual 0 a person's understanding of people, objects, and events.   T F

34. We live life, basically, at the factual level.   T F

35. Most people rarely change their ways of thinking.   T F

36. An allness orientation shows itself usually quite clearly. T F

37. In communicating, you seldom know exactly what others mean. T F

38. You know exactly what I mean when I say, "I love you." T F

39. A non-allness orientation leads to most refusals to listen. T F

40. Even if you don't know or have never met these girls, you can say with confidence that Sally Darling is more beautiful than Madge Zydrovsky. T F

41. Executives who function with a non-allness orientation tend to have more information going from the bottom-up as well as from the top-down. T F

42. Giving symbol reactions usually lead to less jumping to conclusions. T F

43. Most of us tend to respond to the world around us in terms of words and verbal associations than to "facts." T F

44. Scientists need to check their facts just like everyone else. T F

45. Human beings fit the category of "time-binders" more appropriately than the category of "animals." T F

46. You can observe an ordinary lead pencil and rarely names all of the details. T F

47. If they wish, individuals can nearly always misunderstand you. T F

48. In the world of nature, certain things must have natural names rather than made-up names. T F

49. You can find an answer to any question phrased in a coherent sentence. T F

50. Words can affect a person's understanding of people, objects, and events. T F

Introduction

Some ailments fall in the gap between the fatal and the annoying. They represent the precursors of either a more or a less serious state of being. The space between the annoying and the fatal represents a *borderline problem*. Such maladies, disorders, afflictions, or malfunctions consist of just annoying instances, and those who feel afflicted with a borderline ailment often do not take it very seriously. In a world of calamity, tragedy, catastrophe, devastation, misery, havoc, ruin, destruction, and defoliation, possibly we should just ignore borderline ailments. However, to those who experience the persistent gnawing pain of borderline irritations, the annoyance and discomfort may well justify taking direct action. Borderline adversities often impose a gradually deteriorating and damaging impact on the burdened individual.

Nothing seems more futile than offering a solution to someone unaware of a problem!
Loneliness (Riesman, Glazer, & Denny, 1953; Slater, 1970) and **shyness** (Zimbardo, 1977) represent a couple of those borderline ailments and afflictions that often lead to serious depression. So, you feel shy or lonely? So what? Why get irritated about something that you know only represents an annoyance? Little annoyances creep up on most of us, but that don't result in something necessarily fatal. Borderline problems generate somewhat nonspecific effects such as low tolerance of anxiety, poor control over impulses and responses, and an inability to engage in work or hobbies in a meaningful way. Borderline problems seldom show signs associated with psychoses and neuroticisms and other serious mental difficulties, but they do involve many common semantic disorders such as **projection**--seeing our own unpleasant characteristics in others--and **identification**--the process of indiscriminately carrying responses in one situation over to other, different situations, with the assumption that the two situations share identical characteristics, when they reveal quite different features (Johnson, 1946).

Borderline Anhedonia

The term **Anhedonia** refers to a passive joylessness and dreariness, discouragement, dejection, and lack of zest that encompasses a person's demeanor (Stein, 1966). **Borderline** anhedonia describes the experience people have when the situations of their lives stifle their human potential.

Borderline anhedonia does not represent a clinical state like pathological depression, but it may lead to nervous distresses and emotional and semantic disorders of personality such as neuroses, psychoses, and schizophrenia. Sub-categories of such basic disorders as paranoia, manic-depression, involutional melancholia, and the constitutionally psychopathic personality may evolve from borderline anhedonia, depending on the severity of one's life conditions.

The daily use of such expressions as alienation, disillusionment, loss of faith, and lack of respect about what happens to people represent the existence of borderline anhedonia. Borderline anhedonia spreads like a proverbial wild fire, triggering both depression and violence in relationships, with the associated language maladjustments (Castro, 1989).

The daily news regularly reports instances of language disorders that result in emotional outbursts that forebode more intense physical damage (*USA Today,* 1991). The manner in which people talk about their lives, colleagues, workplaces, and what happens to them reveal the seriousness of the indignities they experience. Executives crawl home to hide from the oppressions and obsessions of the workplace, custodians work in silent frustration, teachers and social workers clutch their chairs in white-knuckle anxiety as they prepare to confront clients (Bennis, 1966); parents, university, college, junior college, high school, and, even, middle school or junior high school students become distressed and volatile.

I served for most of my adult life in the role of professor in several universities around the world, in what some consider a highly unlikely occupation and institution for language patterns that indicate either borderline or full-blown disorders to develop (Professor X, 1973). Nevertheless, language usages reveal both rage and indolence in the cells of academia, playing out the consequences of borderline language disorders in the hallowed halls of scholarly institutions. Caplow and McGee (1958), in their analysis of the problems of individual scholars, concluded that "the violent opposition between the academic man's image of himself as a kind of oligarch, independent of lay authority, and the galling subjection which he actually experiences is presumably responsible for the combination of private resentment and public submissiveness that so often characterizes the faculty attitude toward administrators" (228). Little doubt exists that the language of maladjustment flourishes among members of the academic community as well as in communities at large.

Maladjustments Associated with Semantic Responses

For the most part, as our analysis so far suggests, maladjustments, borderline pathologies, and disorders concern much more than just words. Most of our concerns have to do with the structure of sentences and paragraphs and whole expressions and, almost more important, with the ways in which people respond to their own utterances and the utterances of others. Human beings have the capacity to discriminate among alternatives and to adapt as often as they need to, indefinitely and infinitely. Often, however, we just do not seem to feel the need to respond more discriminately nor to use our somewhat natural abilities to adapt.

As we shall attempt to point out later in more detail, we ought to avoid or at least minimize the use of all-inclusive generalizations expressed by terms such as "all," "never," "everything," and "absolutely," but we don't; we should eliminate from our vocabularies—

written and spoken—all forms of the verb "to be," including "is," " are," "was," "were," "am" and "be," but we don't; and we should take special cognizance of the fact that our language utterances more often than not refer to other language statements and we react to our own reactions, rather than reacting directly to events, but we don't.

We shall talk about many more language patterns that lead to disorders of evaluation and maladjustments in our lives. We shall talk about how the process of getting information affects how we think and how we react to the information we create, and how we talk about how we talk about how we react to what we see, and so forth.

We shall talk about "the law of the total situation" that says that people can construct meanings and language patterns that allow them to function in productive and satisfying ways provided they take into account the total situation and avoid denying and distorting cues that allow them to revise their inappropriate assumptions regarding people, objects, and events in the world.

We shall talk about some ideas that explain such puzzles as self-reflecting statements and the question of what one should use as the measurement of success and unravel this conundrum: "If one takes the sword as the best measure of the mind, we reveal little about the mind that makes it different from the sword, but we impose the limitations of the sword on the mind."

We shall contend that our language structure plays a significant role in determining the structure of our society and culture. Thus, we shall argue that a study of language structure may provide insights into and a deeper understanding even of our civilization. As Wendell Johnson once wrote, "Our problem is, in large degree, one of unraveling this net of symbolism in which our human destiny has become entangled" (1946, 18-19). We invite you to pursue this adventure and discover the extent to which you, personally, exhibit critical borderline maladjustments in language use and what you might do to relieve some of the tension created by the way you talk and behave.

Defining Human Beings

Since we plan to talk a lot about being human, we'd like to provide a definition and an idea of what we mean by being human. Most definitions tend to place people in the category as animals, although the highest type of *animals* existing or known to have existed, differing from other high types of animals, especially in their extraordinary mental development. (*Webster*, 1991, 510).

Many also think of human beings as bipedal primate mammals (Homo sapiens) anatomically related to the great apes, but who distinguish themselves especially by the notable development of the brain, with a resultant capacity for articulate speech and abstract reasoning, usually considered to form a variable number of freely interbreeding races (722). Yes, well, maybe so! Would you willingly look at a different way of talking about human beings?

Distinctions among Plants, Animals, and Human Beings

Korzybski explained his definition of human beings in a book called *Manhood of Humanity* (1921) with these paraphrased explications: In analyzing the classes of life, we find three cardinal classes which differ radically in function:

Plants transform solar energy into organic chemical energy. Plants represent a class of life which appropriates one kind of energy, converts it into another kind and stores it up; so we define plants as **chemistry-binders.**

Animals use the highly dynamic products of the chemistry-binding class such as food, whose products undergo a further transformation into a yet higher form. Animals represent a more dynamic class of life which involves the remarkable freedom and power and faculty to move about in space; so we define animals as **space-binders.**

Human beings, like animals have the capacities to bind chemistry and to bind space, but above that, they have the remarkable capacity to summarize, digest, and appropriate the labors and experiences of the past, which neither the chemical-binders nor the space-binders can do. Human beings possess the capacity to conduct their lives in the ever increasing light of inherited wisdom. Because human beings have the natural agency to bring the past into the present and project the present into the future, we define them as **time-binders.** Thus, we deal with three basic categories of living entities: chemistry-binders, space-binders, and time-binders.

Human Beings Elaborated

Korzybski, then, defined humans in terms of what they DO rather than attempting to state what they ARE, thereby declaring a fundamental revision of the 2500 year old philosophic foundation of science, philosophy, and biology. Bois, later, elaborated that concept and referred to human beings as "thinking [C activities], feeling [B activities], self-moving [A activities], electrochemical [X activities] organisms in continuous transaction with a space-time [present, past, future] environment" (1978, 29).

Korzybski suggested that human beings engage in "semantic reactions," which consist of a "single, complex response of *the whole organism*, determined by what the total situation means to the individual at the moment," rather than simple responses to elements in an environment. As human beings, we react "semantically" to what things mean to us at the moment.

Humans as Time-Binders

Humans have the ability to understand the world and to pass that understanding on to future generations. They achieve this by using symbols. People can talk about realities outside of themselves and within themselves and they can talk about their talk.

Korzybski received extensive tributes when he died suddenly in 1950. The primary sentiments expressed attribute Korzybski with formulating a general theory of values that most feel goes beyond sentimental and metaphysical approaches, which received much attention over time. Rather, Korzybski used an engineering, physio-mathematical, approach. He began with an "obvious" fact, but one so large that most people took it for granted and never adequately explored it. Namely, that humans represent a symbol-producing, symbol-using class of life. In other words, the functioning of our symbol systems allows us to regulate our lives and maintain relationships. People live in an environment of symbols, and, for better or for worse, they must live in such an environment, but if they use symbols *intensionally*, the consequences may destroy them.

Our traditional "Aristotelian" educational system makes it difficult for many to understand Korzybski, for it fails to recognize that symbols impose limitations on people and the harsh realities of life come as painful, disintegrating shocks. Cynicism and feelings of hopelessness often result. Korzybski, by contrast, exuded one of the most hopeful and optimistic views of life in which he revealed great tolerance for others and for virtually everything except the refusal of an individual to face reality.

By creating a time-binding class of human beings, Korzybski gave people both stature and dignity within a basically healthy and constructive structure. The concept of human beings as time-binders does not remove, dispute, disparage, or refute any special claims that others hold about human beings. The religious view that human beings descend from spiritual beings and have eternal life finds support in the time-binding concept. The ability to bind time could come directly from the creator of all things. Some have said that the concept of human beings as time-binders represents the most momentous single contribution ever made to our knowledge and understanding of the distinctive nature of people. Korzybski noted that the concept of human beings as time-binders creates the base, the guide, and the source of light for a new civilization.

We'd like to talk about the principles and practices that constitute the base of this new source of light for our time. We intend to bring the explanations of the forbearers of this new philosophy into a more contemporary context and demonstrate its usefulness now. We face some difficulties such as Mike did in this instance.

> *The story goes that a bull chased Pat and Mike across a field one day.*
>
> *Pat scrambled up a tree in the field and Mike ran into a hole. However, a moment later, Mike popped out of the hole and the bull charged him. He dropped back into the hole. Seconds later he popped out again, and the bull charged again.*
>
> *This continued for some time, and, finally, Pat yelled, "Mike, why don't you stay in the hole?" Mike replied, "Well, I'm trying to decide; there's a bear in the hole and the bull outside."*

Our lives may present Mike's kind of dilemma all too often, making life more complicated than what we had planned at the beginning. Nevertheless, we do know that our reactions to events, people, and even objects in the world take on a kind of holistic feeling that probably matches this new idea of a "semantic reaction" rather than just a physical one. We react with more than just our skin; we react with the full complex of electro-chemical, thinking, feeling, and self-moving aspects of our beings. We shall explore issues such as this as we proceed to develop our explanations of reactions to and descriptions of this "semantic" world in which we live.

We want you to approach the application of the principles we discuss in as direct and simple a way as possible. As an approximate analogy, a story going around about test-happy human resource managers may assist you in thinking about simple ways to apply these ideas.

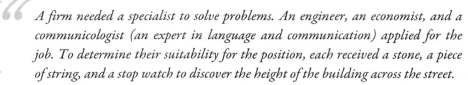

A firm needed a specialist to solve problems. An engineer, an economist, and a communicologist (an expert in language and communication) applied for the job. To determine their suitability for the position, each received a stone, a piece of string, and a stop watch to discover the height of the building across the street.

The engineer took the elevator to the top of roof, tied the stone to the string, and lowered it to the ground. Then he swung it, timing each swing with the watch. With this pendulum, he estimated the height at 200 feet, give or take 12 inches. The economist threw away the string, dropped the stone from the roof, timing its fall with the watch. Applying the laws of gravity, he estimated the height at 200 feet, give or take six inches.

The communicologist, ignoring the string and the stone, entered the building, but soon returned to report the height at exactly 200 feet. How did he know? He gave the janitor the watch in exchange for the building plans. He got the job.

Many of the ideas presented in this book evolve from some rather complex theories, but you might apply them in ways more akin to the way the communicologist did. We shall try to illustrate some of those simple, direct ways as best we can.

Part I: What?

What We Mean by Foolish Ways of Thinking, Speaking, and Behaving!

> *One day one of the greatest bores of a club said to another member,*
> *"I've been grossly insulted. Just as I passed that group over there,*
> *I overheard someone say that he would give me $50 to resign*
> *from the club. "Hold out for a hundred," counseled the confident,*
> *you'll get it."*

How to keep from making a fool of yourself depends, most of the time, on how you think and use language. Johnson explained that whenever enough people or a sufficiently influential group of people approve of something, they establish what we call the normal for that kind of behavior (1946, pp. 338-342). On the other hand, abnormal, or what we consider foolish language use deviates from the normal or average and represents markedly irregular or different from the normal verbal and nonverbal patterns. We tend to regard people who express very unusual or conspicuous actions and whose language patterns deviate enough from the norm as having a high nuisance value. If their views and habits and interests distract from the mores, conventions, and proprieties of members of the society in which that person lives, we consider their verbal and nonverbal behavior as somewhat abnormal.

To discover the most acceptable uses of language and ways of behaving simply challenge the normal uses and see how others react to your so-called deviations from the norm.

> *Two dirty little boys approached a woman walking in a park. The elder of the*
> *two addressed the woman: "Say, lady, me kid brother does some dandy*
> *imitations. Give him a dime and he'll imitate a chicken for you."*
>
> *"What will he do, crow?"*
>
> *"Naw, no cheap thing like that, lady. He'll eat a worm."*

Foolishness versus Reasonable Expectations

Foolish behaviors represent deviations from a norm that others reasonably expect of someone in the social setting in which they live. Here, we try to focus on discrepancies that fall below reasonable expectations for actual language performance. We'll urge you to try not to justify using language patterns that fall below your own potential. If you shrug off deleterious or abnormal ways of talking because making changes seem too difficult to meet the standards of conscientious, serious, well-intended people, you may suffer serious consequences. In other words, normally functioning people should behave consist with valid principles of verbal and nonverbal behavior that they reasonably understand and support. Violating those principles represents gross human inefficiency and leads to maladjustments in interpersonal relationships.

"If a language structure does not fit the facts of experience, then we should expect to find its users talking about what is actually nonexistent, and suffering from delusional states of their own making" (Lee, 1941, p. 117).

Too many of our social policies and educational practices consist of the rehabilitation or custodial care of individuals who engage in maladjusted language behavior rather than attempting to raise the general level of performance in advance so as to avoid developing disorders later (Johnson, 1948). This characterization seems appropriate when, as Johnson explains, we tend to "maintain the status quo of the population as a whole—to keep the drainpipe of civilization in good repair but not to be overly concerned with what comes through it . . . . By diverting our major concern from the drainpipe of civilization to the wellsprings of sanity, we hope to change average [people] from frustrated, tense victims of confusion . . . to clear-eyed, cooperative, creative creatures that [they] seem capable of becoming" (p. 341-343).

Foolish Ways and Maladjusted Language Behavior

Many people have written about and described the most common maladjustments or foolish ways of using language that constitute borderline maladjustments. From a provisional, non-elementalistic, relativistic perspective, we'd like to list some of the primary consequences or problem behaviors that result from inappropriate and inaccurate language uses and common mis-evaluations. The categories represent what results from damaging language behaviors, not bad people, and the categories may not encompass all potential consequences, but they do, hopefully, represent the most common and useful ones for our purposes.

Maladjustments as a Consequence of Inappropriate Language Patterns

Johnson (1948) classified and categorized what he saw as the most common maladjustments in our society, to which inappropriate language patterns lead, including Anxiety, Withdrawal, Aggression, Immaturity, Schizoid or Psychoneurotic and Semantogenic disorders. Bear with us while we briefly characterize each of these categories.

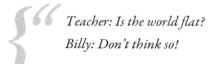

Teacher: Is the world flat?
Billy: Don't think so!

Teacher: Is it round?

Billy: No-o-o-o!

Teacher: What is it?

Billy: My Dad says it's crooked!

Anxiety Tendencies

Billy exhibited some anxiety tendencies, which include worries, fears, and forebodings of various kinds such as fear of the unnatural and real and impending dangers posed by other humans, animals, disease, and storms. "For the most part," Johnson explains, "the anxieties of adults come from perceived attacks on "self-evaluation, social status, and economic security." The failure to maintain self-respect, a good reputation, and sufficient worldly goods generates anxiety that leads to frustration, worry, and loss of self-assurance. Such tendencies result in mild but unsettling uneasiness, fretfulness, worry, and apprehension when trying to approach new people, new situations, and new events (pp. 343-374).

Worry is evidence of an ill-controlled brain;
It is merely a stupid waste of time in unpleasantness.
If men and women practiced mental calisthenics
as they do physical calisthenics,
They would purge their brains of this foolishness.

—Arnold Bennett

Withdrawing Tendencies

Shyness and feelings of inferiority lead to the tendency to withdraw or avoid completely certain situations. When we feel shy around or inferior to others, we tend to avoid them or withdraw from competition or cooperation with them. Such feelings limit our associations, shut off social contacts, and deprive ourselves of experiences that could be beneficial to us. A withdrawing individual does not represent a normal adult; sociability, on the other hand, normal language behavior represents a sign of good health and an adjusted personality.

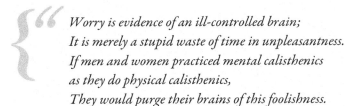

Doctor (after examining her husband): I don't like the looks of your husband, Sally.

Sally: Neither do I, Doc, but he's good to the children.

Aggressive Tendencies

The Farmer and the Cranes
Some Cranes made their feeding grounds on some plowlands newly sown with wheat. For a long time the Farmer, brandishing an empty sling, chased them away by the terror he inspired; but when the birds found that the sling was only

swung in the air, they ceased to take any notice of it and would not move. The Farmer, on seeing this, charged his sling with stones, and killed a great number. The remaining birds at once forsook his fields, crying to each other, "It is time for us to be off to Liliput, for this man is no longer content to scare us, but begins to show us in earnest what he can do."

Frustration and failure in our lives often lead to withdrawal, but, for many, such feelings lead to an exaggerated aggressiveness. Sometimes, aggressiveness results in physical attack, but more often the consequence involves verbal criticism, back biting, argumentativeness, faint praise, and opposition to decisions. Sometimes, aggressiveness takes the form of bullying in the workplace. We also feel that aggressiveness stems from an inability to override obstacles that block our attempts to achieve personal goals. In some cases, however, as illustrated by the Farmer, aggressiveness directed toward overriding an obstacle represents a positive outcome; hence, we think that only aggressiveness with ill-advised and detrimental effects should fall in the category of maladjusted behavior.

Ruler of the House

We measure rooms in our house by Freds. Our living room consists of 3.5 by 2.5 Freds. One Fred consists of 72 inches. As Fred says, "If my wife lost me, she would lose more than just a husband; she would lose two yard sticks".

One may arrive at a Half-Fred by having me lie down and run a chalk line from a point where the top of my head starts as I lie extended along a wall to a point that coincides with my belt buckle. Perhaps it would be easier to buy a tape measure, but in our family, a tape measure can get lost very easily, and, when lost, we can't find it. A misplaced husband will come home when he gets hungry.

Immaturity Tendencies

Immature behaviors tend to develop from one's early or infantile era. Behaviors learned during this early period of time, which consist of primarily nonverbal patterns, tend to exhibit more lasting effects than those behaviors learned later that involve mostly verbal or language behaviors. This seems truer when those learned behaviors elicit pronounced positive effects or powerful discomforts and individuals feel the consequences repeatedly. Adjustment requires a person to evaluate and to unlearn those early infantile reactions to events. Infantilism clearly represents a lack of adaptability in which most people see reactions to events as superficial, irresponsible, impulsive, naïve, selfish, and two-valued, and as Johnson says, they reflect "an exaggerated and unhealthy dependence on others whose authority they take for granted—and with whom they feel themselves to be in actual or potential conflict" (p. 365).

Mark Twain's habit of swearing irritated his wife, who tried her best to cure him of it. On day while shaving, he cut himself. He recited his entire vocabulary

and when he finished, his wife repeated every word back to him. Twain calmly remarked, "You have the words, my dear, but you lack the tune."

Schizoid Tendencies

Schizoid tendencies represent the effects of an inability to meet some idealistic standards to which individuals cling with tenacity. This rigid maintenance of highly personal goals tends to make for a deadly routinized pattern of living plus a definite rigidity of personality structure. Individuals adopt those ideals without considering actual experiences. Such individuals fail to evaluate their beliefs, attitudes, and goals and, as Johnson explains, "they exhibit, in general, the provincial unreflective attitude that people with other ideals and ways of living are somehow queer, uncivilized, or just wrong" (p. 354).

Semantogenic or Psychoneurotic Tendencies

> *A Rabbit on his way to the store came upon a Frog jumping along in a car tire rut; the Rabbit asked the Frog to get out of the rut and go to the store with him. The Frog said, "I can't, but I'll meet you there."*
>
> *As the Rabbit hopped up to the store, there sat the Frog. The Rabbit asked in astonishment, "What happened?"*
>
> *The Frog replied, "A car came along."*

Psychoneuroses, psychosomatic or, in this context, semantogenic disorders reveal themselves mostly through physical symptoms, such as a tendency to feel tired readily. Those afflicted report a regular chronic state of exhaustion while engaged in the simple business of living. They get tired from getting up in the morning, maintaining a few social relationships, and completing personal care tasks. Well-adjusted individuals look forward to working hard, feeling zestful, and performing as outgoing persons. The maladjusted live in a perpetual state of anhedonia or lack of enthusiasm.

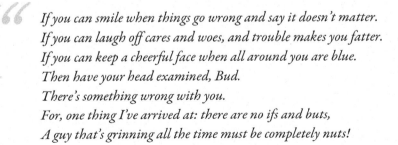

> *If you can smile when things go wrong and say it doesn't matter.*
> *If you can laugh off cares and woes, and trouble makes you fatter.*
> *If you can keep a cheerful face when all around you are blue.*
> *Then have your head examined, Bud.*
> *There's something wrong with you.*
> *For, one thing I've arrived at: there are no ifs and buts,*
> *A guy that's grinning all the time must be completely nuts!*

How to Identify Language Usage Maladjustments

Murray and Barbour (1973) developed a set of guidelines for observing and identifying verbal and nonverbal behaviors that indicate varying degrees of maladjustment. You may recognize language disturbances by two features:

1. **Quantitative deviations** or how often each deviation occurs from a norm measured by the number of times they occur, and

2. **Inappropriate patterns** of behavior such as excessive, extreme, or inconsistent patterns.

Observations of others, as well as of yourself, using these categories should extend long enough to ascertain *patterns* of behavior. Observers should seek to identify words, statements, talk, and writing that regularly and consistently represent disturbances and deviations from the social norm of language use. Murray and Barbour identified three categories of verbal and nonverbal behaviors associated with maladjustments: Those associated with,

1. the process character of reality;
2. the process of abstracting; and
3. language output.

A summary of the definitions of each category and the behavioral manifestations by which one can recognize these maladjustments follow.

Maladjustments Associated with the Process Character of Reality

Category 1: Undelayed or signal reactions that by-pass higher nerve centers. **Behavioral Manifestations**: Impulsive, trigger reactions to conditions, words, things and nonverbal actions; tensions, disturbances, and irritability regarding biases to the point of disruptiveness.

> *Some enlisted men were at bat in a hotly-contested baseball game against their officers when a Private hit what looked like a single to short right field. Instead of stopping at first base, the Private foolishly started a wild dash for second base.*
>
> *Realizing, then, that he couldn't make it to second base, he scrambled back toward first base. Now he was being chased in a run-down between a Lieutenant playing first base and a Colonel playing second base. It looked like a sure out, but just as the Lieutenant flipped the ball back to the Colonel, the Private snapped to attention, saluting the Colonel.*
>
> *Automatically, the Colonel snapped the salute back and muffed the catch, allowing the Private to reach second base safely.*

Category 2: Identifications or confusion of inferences with descriptions or events; behaving as if one were in another place or time, or as if the thing also existed as a word.

Behavioral Manifestations: Mental disorientation or glandular secretion to seemingly disassociated words or word combinations unrelated to present circumstances; arousal and response to only similarities rather than to similarities and differences. Severe reactions to words such as blood, bitch, hospital, homosexual, death, politician, fornication, atheist, or snake.

> *A lady in Florida entertained a group of people for dinner. Everyone was delighted with the meal, although no one could decide exactly of what the main course consisted. After dinner, a man approached the hostess and said, "I enjoyed the food so much that I would like to have my wife prepare the same meal for us. Would you please tell me what we ate?"*
>
> *The hostess replied, "Yes, of course. You just had the pleasure of eating snake steaks.*
>
> *Upon hearing that, the man had the unfortunate experience of seeing his food for the second time.*

Category 3: Uncontrolled Self-Reflexiveness or being unaware that people respond to their own responses.

Behavioral Manifestations: Language statements reinforce one's own angers, fears, and anxieties; exponential building of reactions through mis-evaluations of one's own behaviors so as to reach extremes of hostility, reticence, and neuroticism.

> *A terribly jealous woman used to submit her husband to a regular inspection every evening. The slightest hair discovered on his coat led to the most frightful scene. One night, finding nothing at all, she burst into tears and wept: "Even bald women now."*

Category 4: Allness statements that assume that individual perceptions take into account everything about a person, object, or event. Radical beliefs couched in absolutes, certainties, and finality without doubt or curiosity.

Behavioral Manifestations: The reoccurrence in conversation of the same, fixed ideas, with unspoken or unconscious absolute assumptions and premises that go unchanged in changing situations. Conversations guided by certainty that dogmatically blocks interaction with others.

> *A government clerk received dozens of papers every day, which he was supposed to read and initial. One day a form from another department found its way into his pile. He read it, initialed it and placed it in his out basket. Two days later, the paper came back with the note attached: "This document was not designed for you to handle. Kindly erase your initials and initial the erasure."*

Category 5: Either/Or Evaluations in which a two-valued orientation of "is or is not" choices and options restrict a person's reactions.

Behavioral Manifestations: Gross oversimplifications to the extent that persons seem NOT to be living in a world of process and change; permits invalid polarizations to build in intensity; shuts off consideration of options between assumed polarities, bi-polar tendencies appear to be held unconsciously.

There Are Two . . . .

. . . kinds of people who don't say much—those who are quiet and those who talk a lot.

. . . times in a man's life when he should not speculate—when he can't afford it when he can.

. . . ways to measure honesty in a person—returning a borrowed book or a borrowed umbrella.

. . . sorts of lawyers—the ones who know the law, and the ones who know the judge.

. . . types of movie-goers—those who talk during the film, and those who hush the talkers.

. . . ways to slide easily through life—to believe everything, or to doubt everything.

. . . kinds of voters—those who support your candidate, and a lot of ignorant, prejudiced fools.

Maladjustments Associated with the Process of Abstracting

Category 6: Unsubstantiated Interferences based on insufficient, distorted, or incomplete abstracting; an inability to recognize similarities in differences.

Behavioral Manifestations: Inability to transform sensory and perceptual information into language. Inability to put thoughts into words; inability to translate, paraphrase, and rephrase written and spoken statements into different forms.

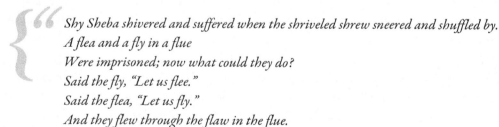

Shy Sheba shivered and suffered when the shriveled shrew sneered and shuffled by.
A flea and a fly in a flue
Were imprisoned; now what could they do?
Said the fly, "Let us flee."
Said the flea, "Let us fly."
And they flew through the flaw in the flue.

Category 7: Undifferentiated Data Focus or the inability to distinguish "here and now" concerns from "there and then" concerns in terms of what topics seem primary and what issues appear secondary; lack of appropriate emphasis.

Behavioral Manifestations: A tendency to perceive crises and routine trivia and exceptional events as pretty much the same. Language statements uttered in terms inconsistent with known facts; habitual lack of consistency. An Inability to see differences in similarities. Primary orientation toward words and definitions rather than what's happening.

> A poultry-raiser (chicken farmer) wrote to the Department of Agriculture: Gentlemen: Something is wrong with my chickens. Every morning I find two or three of them on the ground, cold and stiff, with their feet in the air. Can you tell me what is the matter?
>
> Came back the reply: Dear Sir: Your chickens are dead.

Category 8: Dead-Level Abstracting or the inability to move from basic descriptive levels of events to higher levels of abstracting to allow theorizing, speculation, complex perspectives, or economies of summation. Appears to talk about topics at only a high level of abstraction and without reference to first-order experiences.

> The service-station attendant had changed a tire for me, and as I entered the office to pay the bill, I remarked that it was an awfully hot day.
>
> "How hot is it?" the attendant asked, pointing to the thermometer hanging outside the window.
>
> "It says 85," I replied.
>
> "Well," the attendant noted, "it said 90 a while ago, so I turned the Hose on it. I'm not going to have it that hot around here."

Behavioral Manifestations: Single-mindedness on a topic or persistence in talking on a single level of abstraction, such as at a level represented by words only. Inability to explore a topic in depth. Indifference if a topic shifts from the one under consideration.

Category 9: Inappropriate Evaluations or failure to predict reactions of others; extreme distortions in responses to situations and others; that is, inadequate or excessive and ill-timed or irrelevant, superficial and prolonged responses.

Behavioral Manifestations: Apparent irrationality prevails with inadequate decision-making. Misevaluations subject to emotionality rather than to available factual data. Behaviors out of sync with known facts; fails to refer to available sensory data and avoids or distorts documented information. Lack of concern with effects of decisions on self and/or others. Evaluations not suitable to specific situations.

> Nurse: "How did your friend get such a large lump on his head?"
>
> Joe: "It was because of his bad grammar."
>
> Nurse: "How could that happen?"
>
> Joe: "We were putting in fence posts and he said, 'I'll set this post in the Hole; then when I nod my head, you take the sledge hammer and hit it,' so I did."

Maladjustments Associated with Language Output

Category 10: Under-verbalization or inhibitions resulting from fears or pressures that threatened one's self-image; anxiety about persons or places; lack of spontaneity; avoids relating and interacting with others; avoids exposure and scrutiny during interaction.

Behavioral Manifestations: Avoids leadership or positions of influence or attention. Avoids being included in groups. Retreats from arguments; capitulates or yields in competitive situations. Generalized reticence exhibiting itself in anxious silences of non-personal small talk confined to mundane matters and trivial concerns. Unable to order and employ different patterns of words and usages.

> *One blistering day when the family had guests for dinner, the mother asked her four-year old son to say grace.*
>
> *"But I don't know what to say," the boy complained.*
>
> *"Oh, just say what you hear me say," the mother replied.*
>
> *Obediently, the boy bowed his head and murmured, "O, Lord, why did I invite those people here on a hot day like this?"*

Category 11: Over-verbalization or Inhibitions resulting from highly similar origins as the under-verbalizer, such as resulting from fears or pressures that threaten one's self-image. Feelings of inadequacy and worthlessness; possible anonymity. Excessive and unnecessary talking; use of words to avoid facing problems, to cover up fear, guilt, and anxiety; episodes of incoherency in extreme cases.

Behavioral Manifestations: Compulsive and constant verbalization; excessive demand for "limelight," bidding for attention. Uses words to conceal motivations and incongruities between words and behaviors. Tendency to use lengthy or wordy descriptions to explain "experiences." Unnecessary and excessive qualification; lack of directness and clarity.

> *A lawyer, whose eloquence was of the "spread Eagle" sort, was addressing a jury at length when his legal opponent, growing weary, went outside to rest.*
>
> *Speaking to another lawyer, the first said, "Old Ironsides always makes a great speech; however, if you or I had occasion to announce that two and two make four, we'd just be fools enough to blurt it right out.*
>
> *Not so, Old Ironsides. He would say: "If by that particular arithmetical rule known as addition, we desire to arrive at the sum of two integers added to two integers, we should find—and I assert this boldly, sir, and without fear of successful contradiction—we, I repeat, should find by the particular arithmetical formula before mentioned-and, sir, I hold myself perfectly responsible for the assertion that I am about to make-that the sum of the two given integers added to the two other integers would be four."*

Category 12: Generalized Ego-Centeredness or concern for self, extreme to the point of isolating self from others or maintaining incongruent relations with others. Includes failure to listen for intended meanings of others and tangential responses that serve to disconfirm others as persons of worth.

Behavioral Manifestations: Seemingly involved in conversations with self that exclude others; constrains two-way communication. Defense of one's own image represents the primary concern of the speaker. Superficial attention to and failure to check on mutual feelings. Failure to keep responses relevant to the theme of interaction; unsuitable transitions; interrupts or ignores interaction.

> *A friend was giving a speech to a group of mental patients in the local mental institution. One lady rose in the middle of his talk, addressed the group, and said, "Isn't this the most boring talk you have ever heard? I think it is just terrible." After a few more utterances, she finally sat down.*
>
> *After the meeting, the Director of the Institution approached the speaker and said, "I hope you weren't upset by the woman's outburst. I was quite pleased that she would react at all; she has been here for six months and that's the first sensible thing she's said."*

Category 13: Incongruent Nonverbal Behaviors: Extreme contrasts and incongruity in non-spoken communicative aspects of behavior, particularly when words are expressing one message and nonverbal behavior "mixes" the message or gives another message entirely.

Behavioral Manifestations: Excessiveness and incongruity in dress, grooming, voice, speech patterns, repeated words or phrases; lack of flexibility when inappropriateness interferes with credibility. May involve restlessness and inattentiveness, distraction, and generalized tension.

> *If you tell a man there are 270,453,001 stars in the universe,*
> *he'll believe you, but if a sign says "Fresh Paint,"*
> *he'll have to check it out personally.*

A Cautionary Note

Observers should avoid imputing maladjusted behaviors to those they observe. Murray and Barbour say that "even with the most careful observation, the observers must be constantly aware that they're making inferences about their observations."

> *A lady's husband had been missing for more than a week, and she asked a friend to go with her to the missing person's bureau. There she described her husband as "tall and handsome, with black hair, and pretty white teeth."*
>
> *Her friend gasped, "Why, you know your husband is short, fat, and bald*

and hasn't a tooth in his head."

"Sh-h-h," shushed the wife. "I know, but who wants that back?"

Summary of Key Principles

We may enumerate the specific principles that lead to maladjustments in language use and encourage users to make fools of themselves in terms of some basic actions:

1. Using Signal Reactions
2. Using Identifications
3. Using Unconscious Self-Reflexiveness
4. Using Allness Statements
5. Using Either-Or Evaluations
6. Inability to Distinguish between High-Level and Low-Level Abstracting
7. Inability to Distinguish between Routine Trivia and Exceptional Events
8. Getting Stuck in Dead-Level Abstracting
9. Making Inappropriate Evaluations
10. Excessive Ego-Centeredness
11. Under-Verbalizing
12. Over-Verbalizing
13. Engaging in Incongruent Nonverbal Behaviors

How to Talk Like a Maladjusted Person

To talk like a maladjusted person, you need to confuse levels of abstraction, which allows you to engage in unconscious projections, to overgeneralize routinely, to use unconditional, stereotyped, and undelayed reactions. You may feel relatively tense, resentful and defensive, and fail to distinguish between past and present situations and past and present experiences with people and events. You might react to people and events as if the events shared exactly the same characteristics at all times. You might accept anything presented with sufficient show of authority—of age, precedence, popularity, or financial prestige—and fall prey to unscrupulous advertisers.

Maladjusted people lay their blame for misfortunes more or less indiscriminately on poor loves, allergies, and their innate, inborn deficiencies. Such individuals fail to realize that words and the things they represent exist at different orders of experience and reality. In sum, they simply make fools of themselves (Johnson, 1948, pp. 379-380).

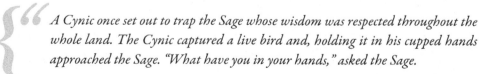

A Cynic once set out to trap the Sage whose wisdom was respected throughout the whole land. The Cynic captured a live bird and, holding it in his cupped hands approached the Sage. "What have you in your hands," asked the Sage.

"A bird," replied the Cynic.

And then he slyly asked, "Is it dead or alive?"

The Cynic thought to fool the Sage, for if the answer were "dead," the bird would be released to fly and thus prove the Sage wrong. If, however, the answer were "alive," the Cynic planned to crush the bird in his hands and exhibit a dead bird.

The Sage looked at the rugged, cupped hands before him and at the cunning face of the Cynic, then calmly said, "It is as you will it."

So can you decide the fate of many of your problems today.

Malfunctioning May Also Occur When You . . . .

1. Fail to distinguish between many-meaning terms and single-meaning terms.

A Pastor approached a congregation committee and asked,

"Where is the chandelier you promised?"

The chair of the committee replied: "We couldn't place the order because,

1ˢᵗ, we couldn't spell chandelier;

2ⁿᵈ, we didn't know whether anyone could play it when it arrived; and

3ʳᵈ, what we need, in any case, is something done about the lights."

For maximum understanding between people, the parties involved must recognize the difference between many-meaning terms and single-meaning terms. The term *to understand*, for example, represents a multiple-meaning term. Seven different meanings appear in the literature, including the idea that understanding means to:

a. follow instructions,
b. make accurate predictions,
c. provide verbal equivalents,
d. undertake agreed on actions,
e. take steps to solve a problem.
f. make appropriate responses, and
g. make proper evaluations.

This seventh meaning involves saying things about the person, object, or event that "fits" them and neither distorts, oversimplifies, overcomplicates, overgeneralizes, negates, adds to, takes from, nor artificially divides them up.

Penicillin tends to represent a single-meaning word that when said or written, it refers to a single substance. So-called "technical" terms tend toward meaning a single thing.

Definitions of what "middle managers" do also include words with multiple meanings:

Middle managers represent the glue that binds the apathy to the vague objectives.

2. Fail to distinguish between statements of "fact" versus statements of "inference."

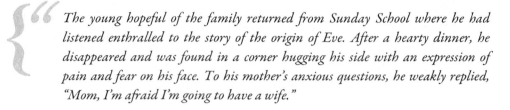

The young hopeful of the family returned from Sunday School where he had listened enthralled to the story of the origin of Eve. After a hearty dinner, he disappeared and was found in a corner hugging his side with an expression of pain and fear on his face. To his mother's anxious questions, he weakly replied, "Mom, I'm afraid I'm going to have a wife."

A "fact" consists of a nonverbal person, object, or event. The moment you say or write something about persons, objects, or events that exist fully and totally nonverbally, you make **statements about them.** For example, one cannot "talk" or "write" a nonverbal happening; all statements simply attempt to describe the nonverbal happenings. Deliberate or accidental inaccurate or false descriptions represent maladjustments in the use of language.

Statements of "fact" or descriptions occur *after* one observes a person, object, or event and the statement represents the observation accurately. Nevertheless, when we realize that every living thing --person, object, or event--consists of moving molecules, we should accept the conclusion that most statements result in a degree of inaccuracy anyway; this means that most statements should reflect some degree of probably that it represents an inaccurate statement.

Statements of inference or guesses occur *prior to* the observation of a person, object, or event or when an observation cannot take place. In addition, you can't predict with more than a degree of probability future happenings. In addition, statements concerning past happenings, where a record of the observation does not exist, should also express the degree of probability that they predict the future inaccurately.

An Elderly stranger entered a little Scottish church carrying an ear trumpet. Never having seen such a Device before, the usher seated the old gentleman with misgivings, then cautioned him, "Ye're welcome to stay, but one toot an' you're oot!

Jumping to Conclusions

We often call the process of confusing descriptive ("factual") statements with judgmental ("inferential") statements, jumping to conclusions. For example, see if you can detect the "inferential" conclusion involved in this incident:

A person's car stopped running near an intersection and another driver stopped and asked if he could help. The driver of the stalled car said, "Why yes, just give my car a push and I think it'll start. However, you'll need to get it up to 40 miles an hour." The car driver giving help backed up a half block and the driver of

the stalled car looked in her rear view mirror just in time to see the helper heading toward her at 40 miles per hour.

3. Fail to recognize that meanings do NOT exist in words.

Listeners often assume that the meaning and the value of a word exists in the word itself; they assume that words have fixed, exact, unalterable meanings. Whereas, in reality human beings assign meanings and values to words. A dictionary, for example, simply attempts to record words used by people and list the variety of meanings imputed to the words. We own dictionaries so that we can find out what meanings other people assign to the words. A dictionary does not dictate or know what a word means. We add new words to dictionaries as they appear in literature and conversations and just record the meanings assigned by the users of the words.

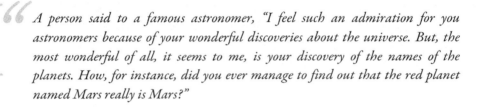

A person said to a famous astronomer, "I feel such an admiration for you astronomers because of your wonderful discoveries about the universe. But, the most wonderful of all, it seems to me, is your discovery of the names of the planets. How, for instance, did you ever manage to find out that the red planet named Mars really is Mars?"

Foolish people assume that the meanings of words exist in the words themselves. Well-adjusted people recognize and seek information about the meanings that people assign to the words they use, rather than assume that they know the meanings. You need to develop tactful ways to inquire about the meanings others assign to their words in your conversations with them.

Preliminary Summary

So far, we listed and explained six borderline ailments and thirteen specific categories of maladies generated by language misuse. We described the specific behavioral manifestations of the misuses so that you can recognize them in your own language behavior. We described how a borderline maladjusted person might so that you might recognize such behaviors in those around you. Finally, we listed and described three statements that reveal additional borderline maladjustments in language use.

Part II: Why?

Why We Lean toward Foolishness!

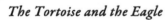

The Tortoise and the Eagle

A tortoise, lazily basking in the sun, complained to the sea-birds of her hard fate, that no one would teach her to fly. An Eagle, hovering near, heard her lamentation and demanded what reward she would give him if he would take her aloft and float her in the air.

"I will give you," she said, "all the riches of the Red Sea."

"I will teach you to fly then," said the Eagle. Taking her up in his talons he carried her almost to the clouds, when suddenly he let her go, and she fell on a lofty mountain, dashing her shell to pieces. The Tortoise exclaimed in the moment of death: "I have deserved my present fate; for what had I to do with wings and Clouds, who can with difficulty move about on the earth?"

Moral: If individuals had all they wished, they would be often ruined.

Problems with Classical Assumptions about Reality and Language

Many of the problems associated with language and thought stem from the early theories and philosophies of the ancient Greeks. Gorman (1962) summarized the characteristics of language as postulated by the primary Greek thinker, Aristotle. She explained that the main features of Aristotelian language-structure have to do with a *subject-predicate structure*, the idea of identity, which involves the assumption that words only have one meaning, *and elementalism* or the practice of dividing up people, objects, and events with words when in reality they represent whole things. We shall review the key principles of the early philosophies to determine more precisely for what they wished to happen and to what ruin they achieved.

Classical Principles of Language/Perception/Reality Relationships
The Principle of Allness

This principle asserts that the word represents the entire object, person, or event. James Snider (1969) translated the concept of Allness into what he called All-Inclusive Conceptualization and published half dozen articles about research on allness. All-inclusive conceptualization represents the tendency to respond to events in terms of over-generalized thinking, responding to an event (internally to oneself or externally to others) that goes beyond the actual verifiable consequences of the event.

David Burns (1980), a psychologist who treats depression, says that "all or nothing thinking and overgeneralization represent two of the "cognitive distortions" that form the basis of all depressions." In Pace's research (1992) on modes of thinking and how people react to unhappy events, three dimensions of all-inclusive conceptualizations or allness thinking emerged: the source or what caused the consequence to occur; the time or how often similar consequences occur; and the space or how extensively the consequences affect one's life.

Three Dimensions of Allness Statements

The way in which we respond to unhappy events reveal three features of over-generalized thinking; making decisions about an unhappy event either internally, to oneself, or externally, to others that go beyond the actual verifiable consequences of the event represents the fallacy of allness statements (See Haney, 1979, Ch. 10, "Allness"). Both initial and sustained reactions to unhappy events show the features of over-generalized thinking and raise three basic questions (Pace, 1992):

1. What caused the consequence to occur (source)?
2. How frequently did similar consequences occur (time)?
3. How extensively did the consequences affect one's life (space)?

These STS dimensions of all-inclusive conceptualization thinking occur when unhappy events affect you. Let us examine these three dimensions in more detail to discover their insidious effects when dealing with unhappy events.

Source Dimension

The first concern in over-generalized thinking has to do with what one perceives as the agent that created the unhappy event, or what one sees as the cause or basic source or reason that explains what precipitated the unhappy event. In terms of a way of thinking about causes, two fundamental causal agents tend to account for unhappy events: our own innate, natural, habitual ways of doing things--**an internal source**, or circumstances independent of us over which we have little or no control, sometimes referred to as others, luck, the environment, or just circumstances--**an external source**.

Internal Sources

When the causal agent that accounts for unhappy events finds its source within us as part of our usual, natural, innate, habitual way of handling affairs, efforts to make changes are often viewed as quite hopeless. When the source of an unhappy event rests in the way in which a person regularly bungles things, the person usually lacks the confidence to find ways to avoid unhappy events. Thus, the person thinks, "Bad things happen because of me. All unhappy events that occur are my fault. I don't have what it takes to do things right." These kinds of statements and thoughts tend to disqualify the person from doing anything good. Hence, we often refer to the thoughts as **disqualifying personalizations** or thoughts that disqualify us as persons.

When the causal agent that accounts for unhappy events finds its roots in the person you think you "are"—your habitual thinking patterns, then the source emerges from your own perceptions of your own abilities as something that naturally keeps you incapable of producing happy consequences. When an event reveals even a small negative consequence, you reveal the tendency to think that the cause of the unhappy event "is" you as a person. Since you brought those tendencies into your life as you came into this world, your birth created the pattern, you can't do anything to create happy events. You as a person create all bad things; you cause bad things to happen; all bad things that occur find their source in your own personal weaknesses.

When something unhappy happens to you, the fault comes from your own being-- yourself—your existence creates bad things. Others or luck or being in a place at the wrong time cannot account for the unhappy event. We identify the cause of unhappy events in our inner thoughts when we think: Nothing *ever* goes the way I planned. I'll *never* make that deadline. I *always* screw up. Again, these statements represent disqualifying personalizations. These kinds of thoughts indicate that your dominate mode of thinking encompasses all-inclusive conceptualizing and accounts for the cause of unhappy events. Everything you plan goes bad; you miss every deadline; you always foul things up. The source of the problem "is" YOU!

External Sources

On the other side of the coin, so to speak, we have people who attribute the cause of unhappy events to factors or circumstances that exist external to or not associated with his or her natural, habitual ways of doing things. This person thinks that unhappy events find their causes in dumb luck, standing in the wrong place, not trying hard enough, or not concentrating on the task. This person's lack of organization occurs because he or she just does not take the time to file things. This person could file things, but he or she prefers to do other things.

Rabbi Kushner (1981) argues that God does not cause bad things to happen, but God does provide support to enable us to deal with the bad things by giving us strength and perseverance. The thought process that you use in making sense out of unhappy events has a distinct possibility of allowing you to cope with unhappy events. We may function better if we think that the sources of unhappy events represent violations of natural laws, failure to perform skillfully enough, a lack of effort or even deliberate decisions by others, rather than our own natural, innate, inherent human deficiencies.

Thinking about the sources of unhappy events as external causes leads us to feel more optimistic. We realize that we can actually take action against the unhappy events or just how we feel about them. We sense that we can deal with them with perseverance and strength and, by doing so, upend the unhappy event and create work that provides meaning and significance to our lives. Eventually, our thinking mode allows us to engage in activities that meet our expectations and fulfill our needs so as to encourage us to perform more effectively and open opportunities for us, giving authentic vitality to our lives.

Most unhappy events, from this perspective, find their source in circumstances and objects and other people over which one may not have control. Bad things come from mis-judgments, from acts of nature, from violations of a principle, from deliberate decisions, and from inadvertent mis-calculations. Rabbi Kushner (1981) attempted to help individuals understand this point of view by explaining that the "laws of nature treat everyone alike. They do not make exceptions for good people or for useful people" (p. 58). Thinking like Rabbi Kushner, who attributes the source of unhappy events to natural processes which may be understood and dealt with and even avoided, we have reason to feel **optimistic** about dealing with unhappy events even though we may not avoid them.

> *A kindly passer-by assisted a small boy in pushing a heavily loaded cart up a long, steep hill. Reaching the top, and at last getting his wind back, he said indignantly, "Only a scoundrel would expect a youngster to do a job like that! Your employer should have known it was too heavy for you."*
>
> *"He did," replied the boy, "but he said, 'Go on, you're sure to find some old fool who'll help you up the hill!' "*

Time Dimension

A second dimension of an all-inclusive conceptual thinking mode has to do with the extent to which unhappy events occur in one's life, identified as a **time** factor. In thinking about unhappy events, one can conceive of them happening constantly, persistently, continuously, and in some stable fashion that reinforces the belief that unhappy events happen to one all of the time, forever and ever, over and over, again and again. This tends to result in **Frozen Evaluations**, which predispose people to respond to disquieting or negative events in their lives in ways that signal feelings of hopelessness.

You can hold an alternative view that says that unhappy events happen from time to time, sometimes, occasionally, or whenever some violation of a social or natural law occurs. Unhappy events fluctuate and happen at various times depending on how things influence your life.

> *At a busy switching station, railway traffic was controlled manually by a watchman. A railroad inspector decided the watchman was a little on the dumb side and decided to test his wits.*
>
> *"Tell me, son," said the inspector, "what would you do if the Midnight Flyer was on time, but the 11:50 Fireball was 10 minutes late?"*
>
> *"Well," reasoned the watchman unhesitatingly, "first, I'd run into my*

shanty there and grab my lunch bucket. Then, I'd run home and git my Grammaw and her rockin' chair; I'd set that chair back there about two hundred feet. And, then, I'd say, 'Set down, Grammaw, and git comfortable, cause in about a minnet yur goin' to see the Dadgumdest train wreck you ever seen."

The theoretical framework of the three dimensions of all-inclusive conceptualization allows you to recognize the sources of hopelessness and pessimistic thinking in your life. Thus, you may find solace in recognizing when you lapse into patterns of thinking that lead to hopelessness, depression, and foolish ways of thinking so you can take action against them.

Continuously. A primary concept in the time factor of all-inclusive thinking assumes that unhappy events happen to you constantly and that they continue to happen many times in the future. You may feel doomed to experience unhappy events continuously. The inner talk that supports the belief that unhappy events happen to you constantly reveals itself in comments such as, "I'm going to foul up again. I will never have opportunities. I am never happy with what I do. Things will continue to go wrong in the future."

Because people feel the way they think, a person who engages in all-inclusive thinking projects a feeling of impending doom in his or her life by predicting that unhappy events will occur in a continuously repeating pattern. If we think that an unhappy event may occur, regardless of what happens, we tend to interpret whatever happens to justify our thinking so that whatever happens appears to have unhappy consequences, thus justifying our thinking.

We often refer to this general way of thinking as the *Pygmalion Effect*, which involves predicting that something will happen and then interpreting events so that their consequences concur or support the prediction. If you think that others will reject a presentation that you plan to make, whatever they say or do may more likely occur in a negative way and end up supporting your assumption that the audience has rejected your presentation.

Occasionally. On the other hand, thinking and conceptualizing that assumes that the conditions of life have a more limited effect on you, so that fewer consequences occur. If you think that negative consequences and unhappy events occur less frequently or only occasionally in your life, you will experience a more positive and optimistic approach to life. Restricting the number of unhappy events in a person's life allows the person to limit the number of negative thoughts and to actually experience fewer unhappy events.

Control over a person's life expands a person's ability to limit the number of unhappy events that occur. Without disregarding reality completely and the possibility of a few unhappy events occurring in some sequence, you can exercise greater control over your life by thinking that unhappy events will in fact occur less frequently, directing your mind to interpret events in a happier framework.

All-inclusive conceptualization involves assuming that you, as a person, have enough control over your life to avoid allowing unhappy events to occur in your life. In addition, all-inclusive conceptualization has a space dimension.

Space Dimension

The space dimension of all-inclusive conceptualization involves thinking that you as a person cause failures in all aspects of your life. You expect unhappy events to happen in all areas of your life, not just at work. The space dimension creates what we call **polarizations.** Making statements like "I am capable of only doing bad things" represent polarizations. When you think that, you feel that unhappy events occur at home, at school, in the community, at church, at the library, shopping, and at recreational events. You think that you will do badly in everything you do. You think that you will be unhappy in everything you do.

Trotter (1987) described the work of E.P. Seligman on depression and concluded that a link between helplessness and achievement may exist, at least as expressed in the ways in which individuals explain their performances. One project with insurance sales representatives indicated that agents with a positive explanatory style--what we called non-allness or limited-conceptualization--twice as often as those with a negative style appeared among those continuing to sell after a year.

All-Inclusive Conceptualizations

A dispirited and pessimistic thinking mode that incorporates **disqualifying personalizations** (a source factor), **polarizations** (a space factor), and **frozen evaluations** (a time factor) predisposes people to respond to disquieting or negative events in their lives in ways that signal hopelessness tendencies. The ability to recognize the three dimensions of all-inclusive conceptualization, the theoretical framework of hopelessness and pessimistic thinking, may aid you in recognizing when you lapse into patterns of thinking that guide your decisions and behaviors toward unproductive and ineffective results.

As Martorano and Kildahl (1989) assert, "inner speech shapes your life more than any other single force. Like it or not, you travel through life with your thoughts as navigator. If those thoughts spell gloom and doom, that's where you're headed, because put-down words sabotage confidence instead of offering support and encouragement." To feel and act with confidence and anticipation, to feel vitality in your life, you need to use a thinking mode that produces confidence, anticipation, optimism, and vitality.

> *An Evangelical adherent attempted to enlist an acquaintance into the fold using a question-answer format:*
>
> *Question: "Are you saved?"*
>
> *Response: "I don't know."*
>
> *Question: "I mean, are you a member of the Christian family?"*
>
> *Response: "No! They live over the hill."*
>
> *Question: "I mean, are you ready for the judgment day?"*
>
> *Response: "When will it occur?"*

Question: "I don't know for sure; it could be tomorrow or the next day."

Response: "When you find out, let me know; my wife will probably want to go both days."

Recognize, identify, and reduce all-inclusive conceptualizations in your inner and outer speech. Consider the source; recognize and talk about the source of unhappy events in terms of the external circumstances that caused them. Do not allow yourself, your personal being, to be the cause. Find other causes and talk about the causes as circumstances that you can overcome, avoid, or make non-existent in your life.

Consider the time: recognize and talk about the cause of unhappy events in terms of limited, restricted, narrow consequences. Make certain that both your inner and outer speech indicates that the causes of unhappy events result in just this one, particular unhappy consequence. If you do as we suggest, you will make progress toward a Non-Inclusive Conceptualization of reality and talk and write and think in a more adjusted manner.

The Principle of Identity/ Predication

A subject-predicate language best expresses this view in such sentences as, "The leaf is green." or "The boy is strong." This tendency—to regard objects as static and the qualities of the objects as inherent in the objects themselves—results in the tendency to stress similarities and to ignore differences in people, objects, and events. The idea of focusing on similarities results in the practice of classifying objects, people and events. Concurrently, this practice of focusing on similarities and creating categories lead to the belief that objects of a certain class are identical or all alike in every respect: Thus, one could say, "Man is an animal," a classification that has persisted over time. If "man" is an animal, then man shares all of the characteristics of "animals."

Most leaders in the field think that the subject-predicate structure of sentences in Indo-European languages predisposed people to use the verb "is," which implements the "is of identity." Identity means "absolute sameness in all respects of two entirely different entities." In Aristotelian thinking, identify means that whatever you say it is, it exists that way. If I say "You are stupid," Aristotelian thinking accepts your state of existence as fully and completely "stupid." You exist that way and you can't change.

The verb "to be", however, means at least four different things:

1. As the auxiliary verb: It is raining; translated, it means, the rain falls.
2. As the "is" of existence: I am; translated it means, I exist.
3. As the "is" of predication: The rose is red; translated it means, the rose looks red.
4. As the "is" of identity: The rose is a flower; translated it means, the rose fits into the classification of flower.

The first two uses (auxiliary and existence) often seem difficult to avoid in popular, everyday English usage, and they may seem relatively less important than the other two uses, which represent critical errors in describing reality or the way things actually exist.

The *Is* of Predication

We call the first critical error **predication**, which involves the use of the verb to be that leads to false statements. If, for example, we say, The Rose **IS** Red, we must realize that redness does not exist in nature. Red consists of only different wave lengths of radiation. Our reaction to those light waves represents only our individual reactions, not a universal condition of existence. "Color-blind" individuals may have "gray" reactions, rather than our so-called "red" reactions. We must realize that to say, the Rose Is Red represents a false statement. We may correctly say, "We see the rose as red." This represents the phenomenon of predication or projection, in which one projects an attribute, an internal evaluation, onto an outside "reality." When you feel angry, you accuse the other of feeling angry and say, "You are angry." Any statement that you make using the "is" of predication or projection cannot express accurate perceptions; all "is of predication" statements represent false statements. To achieve accuracy in language usage, we must scrub those kinds of statements out of our vocabulary.

Suppose you have a negative reaction toward something, how would you describe your reaction? You might say, "That object is obnoxious." That represents an Is of Predication. A more accurate reaction and description of the reaction might say, "I get upset when I look at that object." You remove the projection by assuming responsibility for the reaction and labeling it one of your reactions. The object does not acquire an attribute; rather, you describe your own feeling about the object.

The *Is* of Identity

We call the second critical error, **identity**, which involves the use of the verb to be to make false statements. Korzybski took the conditioning process of behavioral psychologists as a point of departure in explaining the source of identity. He insisted that acquiring language habits through conditioning leads to "false-to-fact semantic reactions. When a word becomes a conditioned response to the thing it represents, the user identifies the word with the thing. Thus, we react to the thing by stating its name and then reacting to the name as if the thing and the name existed identically in every respect. However, we know that the word or name exists separately from the thing being named. You and your name consist of totally different realities. You can put your name on a sheet of paper, but you stand separate from both the name and the paper.

An interesting question may reveal the relationship of words to things. We occasionally ask, "How did Sir Arthur Fleming know that he had discovered penicillin?" The answer, of course, says that Fleming did not know that he had discovered penicillin. He discovered a mold and named it penicillin. To follow the logic of this answer, you need to understand that reality and perceptions come first and words or names follow. A tree exists first and we give it a name second. Naturally, you can imagine things first and give the imagining a name afterward. Light blazes through the sky and you call it lightening. You have a somewhat rectangular object with square features jutting up in front of you, and you ask, "What name did they give to that object." A friend says, "We call it a keyboard." The object came first and we gave it a name second.

How to Avoid the Effects of Subject/Predicate Patterns

The first step toward avoiding making a fool of yourself involves acquiring the habit of **delaying your reactions** to a word or a thing until you can restructure the sentence or reaction so that it represents (symbolizes) more accurately the structure of the reality. This delayed reaction represents a denial of the principle of identity—that A is A or the object rose is identical with the name rose--which they are not. More accurately, identifications need to be recognized as reactions of classification. That is, the more accurate statement for the utterance, "A rose is a flower" would be "I classify the rose as a flower." This is structurally correct and implies that our nervous system and we as people do the classifying.

In keeping with Aristotle's theory that language represents an outgrowth of man's view of the universe, Aristotelian language results from a pre-scientific attitude in which observers, without scientific instruments, thought they saw stable objects with changing qualities inhering in or belonging to them.

The whole idea of classifying people, objects, and events led to the belief that those things all have an unchanging substance and exist as static entities, always the same and never changing. Eventually the idea of identity led to the belief that words and the things to which they referred were the same. For example, if I said that you were "beautiful," you became that attribute. On the other hand, if I said that you were "stupid," you became that attribute. Whatever I said it was, it existed that way all the time, without deviation. Once classified, you could not acquire any other attributes. So, if I called you a "nerd," you continue as a nerd forever; if I call you an "athlete," you carry that attribute all of your life, even when you can't jump a foot or walk a mile.

The two-valued orientation developed from the law of identity, because it represents merely another expression of the **"law of the excluded middle."** That law says that whatever is, is itself absolutely, and goes on to say that words are things. Symbols are equated with what they represent; the two sides of the semantic equation are equivalent. There can be no middle ground—a thing either is, or is not. The rigidity, totalitarianism and authoritarianism of the Aristotelian orientation resulted in the practices of identity and the two-valued orientation, which asserts that a thing exists as either black or white, good or bad, true or false. The corollary **"law of contradiction"** says that a thing cannot be and not be at the same time so that a man cannot occupy two different categories at the same time.

Recognize Genuine Dichotomies

Contradictory Terms. Some categories place people, objects, and happenings in genuine dichotomies such as an airplane flying at higher than 6,000 feet versus an airplane flying at an altitude lower than 6,000 feet. Such situations provide clear-cut distinctions with mutually exclusive categories. You might think of other true dichotomies, such as a chair or a wall, a computer or a shovel, a street or a house, and so on.

Contrary terms. The *space* dimension of allness thinking leads to what we call **polarizations,** such as making statements like "I am capable of only doing bad things." Such a statement *creates* the dichotomy of either good or bad. The question raised by polarizations concerns whether the categories represent mutually exclusive differences or do they represent scales from one side to the other? For example, to say that people occupy fully and completely only one end of a scale from good to bad raises questions. May people exhibit both good and bad behaviors or appearances or attributes? In fact, people may exhibit neither good nor bad of anything, since good and bad represent statements that impute characteristics onto people rather than separate them into categories. For example, this bit of verse, the source of which having long since disappeared, expresses **the contrary idea:**

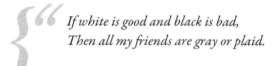

> *If white is good and black is bad,*
> *Then all my friends are gray or plaid.*

Most references to attributes of people actually represent contrary statements, rather than contradictory ones. To demonstrate the ease with which our language structure allows us to make contradictory dichotomies out of contrary scales, study the following list of dichotomous terms while applying the attributes to a specific person whom you know well. Can you divide these attributes into genuine mutually-exclusive categories?

> *Either large or small?Either beautiful or ugly?*
> *Either strong or weak?Either clean or dirty?*
> *Either calm or agitated?Either young or old?*
> *Either brave or cowardly?Either honest or dishonest?*
> *Either relaxed or tense?Either happy or sad?*
> *Either wealthy or poor?Either healthy or ill?*
> *Either competent or incompetent?Either intelligent or stupid?*
> *Either fast or slow?Either kind or cruel?*
> *Either fair or unfair?Either cautious or rash?*

We could extend the list for a long time, but these examples should show the difficulty of accurately placing anyone on only one pole of each of these dichotomies. Clearly, the attributes of people fall somewhere along the continuum between both characteristics rather than conveniently at one end or the other. The failure of our language to include detailed gradational terms tends to encourage us to create polarities and talk about contradictory events where they actually represent contrary situations.

To demonstrate the difficulty of talking in terms of middle-grounds, complete the following two-tier exercise:

Exercise

Instructions: As quickly as possible, list the opposites of the following terms:

Clean . . . . ._____

Strong . . . . ._____

Young . . . . ._____

Brave . . . . ._____

Beautiful . . . . ._____

That didn't take too much effort, did it? Generally, we can think of the opposite of such terms as tall or young rather easily.

Now, fill-in the appropriate gradational terms between the "opposite" words listed above. Begin with the center column and proceed to the columns on each side only after completing the center space.

How did you feel about the second task? Did you complete all three of the lists? Did you think of some words that actually express one or more steps along the continuum between Clean and Dirty? We often use the term Gray to refer to the middle position between White and Black, but what about the other gradations? Possibly the term, Comely, came to mind to describe the point between Beautiful and Ugly, but what about the other points on the scale?

To avoid polarizing too often, we occasionally use expressions such as "a little less than" or "a little more than", but this circumlocution seems so inadequate that we just go to the unqualified polar term and "let it go at that." Such an attitude doesn't mesh well with attempts to do your best or to avoid making a fool of yourself. You need to regularly convert *polarisms* into the more accurate *contrary* form and work diligently to find terms that express refined positions on the scale.

From our discussion of the structure of reality, we concluded that reality consists of an infinite number of highly differentiated particles, each unique and individual. On the other hand, language consists of a limited number of words. A crucial difficulty arises from our attempts to represent a reality of boundless differences with a language having a limited number of words. Even though a dictionary may contain 1664 pages of words and definitions, we stand very far from having one word for each different particle, object, person, and event in the world. We talk about a considerably larger number of things—people, objects, and events—than we have words available to describe them. This means that we must use the same words to refer to different things. For example, the term *knowledge* may refer to the reaction you get from holding the positive terminal of an electric circuit in your right hand while at the same time you hold the negative terminal in your left hand—ZAP--, or from reading a book, or from watching two chipmunks play on a pile of logs, or from any number of different experiences.

The convenience of encompassing a gross variety of happenings under a single word may offset the disadvantage of the potential confusion that could arise from trying to give every sensation and reaction a different name. Nevertheless, with a restricted number of words at our command and an infinitely varied reality to describe, maybe you can see why language symbols can never correspond exactly with the realities they attempt to describe.

> *A young salesman asked in a faint voice, "You don't want to buy any life insurance, do you?"*
>
> *"I certainly do not," the sales manager replied.*
>
> *"I thought you didn't," the embarrassed salesman uttered, and headed for the door.*
>
> *Then the sales manager called him back and addressed him sternly, "My job is to hire and train salesmen, and you're about the worst salesman I've ever seen. You'll never sell anything by asking people if they don't want to buy. But, because you're apparently just starting out, I'm going to take out $10,000 worth of insurance with you right now. Get an application blank."*
>
> *Fumbling, the salesman did so, and the deal was closed. The sales manager said, "Another word of advice, young man. Learn a few standard organized sales talks."*
>
> *The young salesman replied, "Oh, I've already done that. I've got a standard talk for every type of prospect. This is my organized approach for sales managers."*

An equally perplexing difficulty arises from the circumstance in which many different words refer to the same event. A thesaurus of words often records a multitude of terms that can be used to refer to a single act. For instance, for the act of "moving quickly," you have the terms run, sprint, dash, scurry, scamper, gallop, and lope at your disposal. Thus, if two individuals observe the act of moving quickly, they may select quite different words to describe what they thought they saw.

> *A young fellow broke his leg skiing, and the doctor told him that he couldn't use the stairs until the leg had healed (the fellow's bedroom was on the second floor). A few months later, the fellow returned to the doctor's office and had the cast removed.*
>
> *The doctor asked him how he felt about the leg.*
>
> *The skier asked, "This is just fine; is it all right for me to use the stairs now, I'm awfully tired of climbing up the drain pipe to get to my room?*

Elementalism

This concept addresses the tendency of either-or language to divide aspects of reality that actually comprise a scale and simply represents different aspects of the same thing. For example, Einstein taught us that *time* and *space* represent different aspects of the same phenomenon and should be expressed as time-space. For example, elemental thinking says that we exhibit exclusively emotional problems, whereas most of our problems share both intellectual and emotional aspects, arguing that we should talk about psycho-logical difficulties.

Elemental thinking tends to imply that highly interdependent, constantly moving, ordered relations that exist at the silent level of reality actually exist as absolute, non-related, independent entitles or elements.

These tendencies tend to be perpetuated by primitive and animalistic concepts of reality and impose a form of infantilism on our institutions, educational methods and doctrines. These conditions, in turn, produce leaders afflicted with their own animalistic, non-scientific, primitive limitations (Korzybski, 1933, Einstein, Heisenberg, and Eyring as summarized by Bronowski, 1953). The principle criticisms of Aristotelian thought say that it perpetuates *the inaccurate notion of substance and a definite order of existence*, along with the *notion of essence* or the idea that things possess attributes that do not change.

The Principle of Self-Reflexiveness or Circularity

 How does implementing the principle of self-reflexiveness tend to make you a fool? Even our references to non-allness reflect the self-reflexiveness of language: "Never and always" represent two words one should always remember never to say." Always avoid "always". Never say "Never." These self-contradictory statements create confusion, until we recognize that the same word is used on different levels of abstraction.

> *An artist was in a field painting, with a farmer watching him.*
>
> *The artist remarked, "Ah, perhaps you too are a lover of the beauties of nature. Have you seen the golden fingers of dawn spreading across the eastern sky, the red-stained, sulphurous clouds at midnight blotting out the shuddering moon?"*
>
> *The farmer replied, "No, not lately, I've been on the wagon for over a year!"*

The principle of self-reflexiveness asserts that a map of an area that purports to represent the area should include the person drawing the map, an essentially impossible task. Applied to everyday interaction, we say that language can be used to talk about language or that language allows us to engage in self-reflexiveness. We must realize with a strong feeling that self-reflexiveness contributes to language maladjustments.

> *Father, rocking howling baby, says, "Easy now, Danny. Keep calm. Steady there, Danny. It's okay, Danny boy."*
>
> *Passerby comments: "My, you're patient with that child. What's the matter with*

little Danny?"

Father, replies, "He's Christopher. I'm Danny."

Self-referring propositions, such as "all statements in this box are false," represent a form of self-reflexivity and the contradictions that occur. Humor often reveals self-reflexiveness: Bob Hope explained that the automobile industry invented a remarkably new automobile, which simply required you to push a button that pushed a button that pushed a button to operate it. George Burns, a comedian, once told of his uncle's invention designed to deal with the removal of spots left by spot removers.

> *So many times a small action by one individual can bring repercussions upon many. For example, the boss at work has a small row with his wife at home. He comes to the office feeling slightly put out, and Joe pulls a booboo. The boss retaliates upon Joe. That evening Joe returns home from work. The wife is slightly behind schedule in preparing dinner, and Joe, good boy that he is, becomes aggravated, and exchanges words with the little woman. She is taken by surprise, but nonetheless is shaken up.*
>
> *Junior just happens at that time to spill a bit of food around the vicinity of his chair as per usual, but Mom just raises Cain this time.*
>
> *Well Junior, being understandably frustrated, gets off his chair and goes into the other room, where Rover is lying peacefully on the rug. Junior, for no apparent reason, kicks Rover where it hurts. Rover then, in a very misunderstood manner, immediately takes his pain out on the poor innocent kitten. The tremors continue innumerably.*

Suppose you attempt to describe your current situation. Obviously, if you attempt to describe your current behavior, you must also describe you describing yourself describing your current actions, and so forth. Likewise, much of our thinking and talking involves thinking and talking about what we thought and talked about. In fact, you may talk about how you feel and then feel something different because of the talking you did about the new feeling. We say, "I should have said," or "Aunt Millie said that she heard Uncle Billy say that Cousin George said that Maxell said that we ought to vote for Steve." In daily conversations with one another, we constantly talk about what the other person said, sometimes to get clarification, but most of the time just to talk. The entire process of communicating involves constant and numerous examples of the self-reflexive nature of language.

You should seek as complete an awareness as you can of the damage that self-reflexiveness does in your daily language interactions. Constantly ask yourself the question, "Am I engaged in talking about my own talking or responding to my own responses rather than responding as directly as possible to the responses of others as calmly as I can?"

An Infinite Regress that Reinforces One's own Angers and Fears

One serious consequence of self-reflexiveness in language results in the unnecessary and often deleterious reinforcement of one's own feelings. Expressions such as, "I feel angry because I feel angry because I feel angry," illustrate the devastating piling-on of layers of feelings that move innocent reactions into voluminous and magnified emotional skyscrapers. You would not likely allay a fear or reduce a response of anger through self-reflexing your feelings of anger or fear; you would more than likely intensify the feelings, potentially resulting in devastating consequences. Many people have reacted violently as a result of building layers of emotions through the self-reflexive process. Maintaining control and oversight of your own self-reflexing tendencies may very well represent one of the most important successes in your live. It may save you from making a serious fool of yourself.

> At Dublin's Abbey heater, poet-playwright, W.B. Yeats was looking for realism in creating the lighting effects for a glorious sunset. Hour after hour he had the electricians try every conceivable combination of colors and rheostats. At last he saw exactly the effect he wanted. "That's it!" he cried. "Hold it, hold it!"
>
> "We can't hold it, sir," came a stagehand's apologetic voice, "The bloody theater's on fire."

Incomplete Descriptions

The structure of our language, the structure of the world, and the structure of our nervous systems appear to prohibit any complete, final, kind of description, since human symbolizing involves an indefinite self-reflexiveness. In reality, we cannot make an absolutely complete statement due to the self-reflexive characteristic of perceptions, abstracting, and symbolizing. We may explain this anomaly by the fact that when a person attempts to describe a situation or make statements about another person, object, or event, the person describing the situation exists in the situation being described and, therefore, the describer becomes self-reflexive and must describe him or herself.

Multiordinal Terms

Self-reflexiveness and Multiordinality share a common experience in that they derive their meanings from different levels of abstraction. To explain in another way, multiordinal terms, without changing their dictionary definitions, mean differently at different levels of abstraction. Terms such as "love," "beautiful," "courage," "truth," "meaning," "problem," and "management" have different meanings when used as first order descriptions and when used as fourth order descriptions. For example, when you say, "I have a problem," what do you mean? You cannot give a general answer to such a question because the answer depends on the level of abstraction and the context in which the term finds its application.

You may say, "My big toe hurts," and such a problem exists at a near first-order of abstraction, or you may say, "The government has infringed on my freedom," a statement that gets its meaning from a fourth or higher order of abstraction. The dictionary definition of a problem—a barrier to achieving a goal—remains the same for both statements, but the meaning depends on the level of abstraction.

Instructions:

In the space provided, write a one-sentence or phrase reaction to each statement; do not give much thought to what you write; make your reaction quite spontaneous.

1. Pine furniture is the best kind.

_____

2. I do not understand why anyone likes the color blue.

_____

3. The legal voting age should be set at 21 years.

_____

4. You are too tall.

_____

5. Playing dominoes is a fantastic sport.

_____

6. Everybody should eat wheat germ.

_____

7. Humanities class is a waste of time.

_____

8. The number 13 should never be used.

_____

Analysis: What kinds of reactions did you give to the statements? Why? Could the meaning of each statement change in a different context? Some of the sentences used the "IS" verb, such as 1, 4, 5, and 7 while others did not, such as 2, 3, 6, 8. Did you notice that just about every statement involved making some judgment? Do multiordinal terms tend to involve judgments more than other types of statements? Why?

Multiordinal terms have a central place in communicating, since they facilitate the resolution of some difficult misunderstandings stemming from some very abstract statements. The meanings emerge from the self-reflexiveness and multiordinality of the terms used. To understand such a statement requires you to make clear the context in which you assert the condition of having, for example, a problem. The term "problem" means different things at different orders of abstraction. You can have "problems" at the "hurt" level, at the "someone doesn't like me" level, at the "country takes my freedom away" level, and so on.

The apparent shifting of meanings for a multiordinal term shouldn't bother us, since it allows flexibility in interpreting the meaning of expressions and leads to the mutual discovery of the contexts in which we use words and promotes accuracy of statement and, eventually, agreement. The whole process requires an awareness of orders of abstraction and how we evaluate things. Such understandings tend to counteract disabling and maladjustment stemming from worry, fear, resentment and anxiety.

> *Waiting in line at an ice-cream stand were two boys—7 and 2. The little one was announcing emphatically to all the world, "I want vanilla, I want vanilla!"*
>
> *Knowing how two-year olds react, I wondered how the older boy would handle the situation when he discovered that the vanilla was all gone. Without flinching, he ordered two strawberry cones and handed one to his little brother. "Here you are," he said, "Pink Vanilla."*

Lack of awareness of self-reflexiveness and multiordinality

A lack of awareness leads to maladjustments associated with rumors, gossip, daydreaming, suspicions, and delusions resulting from the mistaken assumption that words have simple and clear definitions and meanings. An awareness of multiordinality and self-reflexiveness allows us to abandon the attempt to assign a *general* definition to terms and devote our time to making clear the context from which terms derive their meanings. We would no longer dispute over what terms such as love," "beautiful," "courage," and "kindness" mean and devote our time to specifying the context from which the terms derive their meaning.

Initial Summary

In Part II we talked about why we tend to engage in making foolish statements. We attributed some of the tendency to the classical principles of Allness, Identity, and Self-Reflexiveness. We talked some about disqualifying personalizations, frozen evaluations, polarizations, predication or projection, identity, contradictions and contraries, infinite regresses, and multiordinal terms. The consequence of making some of these deviations from the norm part of your everyday conversation may lead to misunderstandings and the emergence of some borderline disturbances. In the next Part, we shall attempt to focus on ways of talk that encourage us to think, evaluate, and talk more accurately and less foolishly.

Part III: When?

When do We Start Using a More Contemporary Approach?

People should never feel ashamed to own that they behaved wrongly, which just demonstrates, in other words, that they behaved more wisely today than they did yesterday.

Paraphrased from Jonathan Swift

New Models of Reality, Perceptions, and Symbols

In contrast to the beliefs of Classical scholars, scientists postulate that we actually live in six different "worlds" or levels of matter. Understanding these differences should make a difference in the way we talk, write, evaluate, and respond to reality—people, objects, and happenings. Let's look at each of the six levels for a few minutes.

Six Worlds of Matter

1. Nuclear or Sub-Microscopic. The first world consists of the *atomic nucleus*, the nucleus where most of the weight of an atom exists and has a diameter less than one ten-thousandth that of the atom. Vibrations inside the nuclei of atoms move around about a million times more frequent than the vibrations between atoms. *Time* Magazine (Kluger, 2013) reported that research scientist Ms Fabiola Gianotti, a leading scientist at the Large Hadron Collider (LHC), in a facility on the border of France and Switzerland, had confirmed the Peter Higgs theory that "particles live in a field with which they interact. Those interactions give particles their mass, basically by attracting Higgs bosons to them. The more they attract, the greater their mass."

The LHC consists of an instrument 151 feet long and 82 feet high and equipped with a massive magnet system that allows the paths of charged particles to bend so they can be measured. The machine/instrument weighs 7,000 tons. The LHC works in connection with a piece of hardware known as the liquid-argon calorimeter, which detects electromagnetic energy. The machine responds in less than 50 billionths of a second, and detects particles moving close to the speed of light. Higgs' theory has acquired prominence because a particle doesn't necessarily have to have mass; the photon, the basic quantum of light, doesn't have mass. If no particles had mass, however, the universe, along with everything in it, would function decidedly differently and appear less solid. The Higgs particle—a boson—has two functions. One gives mass to particles and the other allows the standard particle to behave properly up to the highest energies (*Time,* December 31-2012-January 7, 2013, pp. 128, 130).

We appear to have learned more about the smallest and fastest particles that comprise the world of reality in which we live than we might digest in one setting. I personally find it difficult to comprehend particles of the earth moving at 50 billionth of a second. That's faster, of course, than a speeding bullet.

2. Atomistic. The second world comprises the world of *atoms and molecules.* This still represents a very tiny world. It would take just 100 million atoms placed side by side to reach an inch. A molecule finishes one of its vibrations in about a ten million millionth of a second. For lack of a better term, we call this a "Jiffy."

3. Perceptual. The third world comprises the world of *everyday life.* Here we measure time in seconds or minutes and distances in feet or miles. We know the most about this feature of the world.

4. Solar. The fourth world has to do with the *astronomical* world. By using the largest telescopes, we can see out so far that the light reaching our eyes started on its journey toward us almost two and one-half billion years ago.

5. Cosmic. The fifth world consists of the fields of existence beyond the telescopic or what we can see with our most powerful instruments that probe the universe. We know hardly anything about this world, but we hypothesize its existence as a result of what we see with our current telescopes, but we anticipate that we shall invent even more powerful instruments that take us into the cosmic world a bit farther.

6. Spiritual. The sixth world goes by the name, the *spiritual* world, which consists of "refined" matter. We know almost nothing about how the spiritual world operates, but it no doubt functions faster, quicker, and farther than anything about which we know at the moment. Like the other worlds that we can't perceive with our current senses, the spiritual world most likely exists at another level of perception. The eternal laws that govern the spiritual world may require some extended time, running into eternity, to discover and understand.

Living in a world in which particles move at 50 billionths or 10 million millionth of a second and travel three billion miles and take 100 million atoms to reach an inch, we must realize that our whole world consists of things in motion. It seems obvious that everyone should recognize that such movements must be taken into account when we attempt to represent the people, objects and events in the world with language.

Writing in his book on *Abnormal Psychology and Modern Life,* James Coleman notes:

> *"With the advent of the space age, man is confronted with a new perspective of time and space, and the problem of finding the meaning of his existence in a universe in which he earth and even the whole solar system may be no larger in relation to the whole as an atom is to the earth. At the same time, materialistic values—based on the belief that scientistic progress would automatically lead to man's happiness and*

fulfillment—have proved sadly disillusioning. As a result, many people are groping about, bewildered and bitter, unable to find any enduring faith or to develop a satisfying philosophy of life. Despite their fine automobiles, well-stocked refrigerators, and other material possessions and comforts, the meaning of life seems to be evading them. In essence, they are suffering from existential anxiety—*deep concern about finding values which will enable them to live satisfying, fulfilling, and meaningful lives.*

Searle (1995) explains the distinction between **Intrinsic and Observer-Relative Features of the World.** His distinctions provide some important differences between the composition of reality and our perceptions of reality. His discussion may seem a bit esoteric, but it does provide an explanation for why we can make a distinction between "reality" and our "perceptions" of reality. Intrinsic reality exists independent of our perceptions of it. Searle doesn't write in E-prime English, so you should feel free to translate any instances of "to be" used by Searle so that it represents action rather than passive verbs. The following represents a paraphrase of Searle's analysis:

> The features of the world I described in characterizing our fundamental ontology, e.g., mountains and molecules, exist independently of our representations of them. However, when we begin to specify further features of the world, we discover that there is a distinction between those features that we might call *intrinsic* to nature and those features that exist relative to the *intentionality of observers, users, etc.* It is, for example, an intrinsic feature of the object in front of me that it has a certain mass and a certain chemical composition. It is made partly of wood, the cells of which are composed of cellulose fibers, and also partly of metal, which is itself composed of metal alloy molecules. All of these features are intrinsic.

But it is also true to say of the very same object that it is a screwdriver. When I describe it as a screwdriver, I am specifying a feature of the object that is observer or user relative. It is a screwdriver only because people use it as (or made it for the purpose of or regard it as) a screwdriver.

The existence of observer-relative features of the world does not add any new material objects to reality, but it can add epistemically objective *features* to reality where the features in question exist relative to observers and users, and so we regard the features as ontologically subjective.

1. The sheer existence of the physical object in front of me does not depend on any attitudes we may take toward it.

2. It has many features that are intrinsic in the sense that they do not depend on any

    attitudes of observers or users. For example, it has a certain mass and a certain chemical composition.

3.   It has other features that exist only relative to the intentionality of agents. For example, it is a screwdriver. To have a general term, I will call such features "observer relative." Observer-relative features are ontologically subjective.

4.   Some of these ontologically subjective features are epistemically objective. For example, it isn't just my opinion or evaluation that it is a screwdriver. It is a matter of objectively ascertainable fact that it is a screwdriver.

5.   Although the feature of being a screwdriver is observer-relative, the feature of thinking that something is a screwdriver (treating it as a screwdriver, using it as a screwdriver, etc.) is intrinsic to the thinkers (treaters, users, etc.). Being a screwdriver is observer-relative, but the features of the observers that enable them to create such observer-relative features of the world are intrinsic features of the observers.

Conclusion: Observer-relative features exist only relative to the attitudes of observers. Intrinsic features don't give a damn about observers and exist independently of observers. That is, **intrinsic features of reality are those that exist independently of all mental states**, except for mental states themselves, which are also intrinsic features of reality (10-11).

To describe, characterize, and accurately represent what happens on the earth requires some dramatic changes in the ways we think about and talk about happenings around us. We must re-think how we talk accurately about such an exciting environment. Such a change may represent the most critical, dramatic, exciting and essential departure from traditional ways of seeing and understanding happenings in the world.

At minimal, we know that to represent such fantastically moving particles, our language must take on a more provisional character. Talking about things in ways that represent them inaccurately only leads to confusion, misguidance, and malfunctioning. As users of language, we must reject as inadequate the assumption that we can explain completely and predict flawlessly human behavior. In the world of reality, as we see it today, events occur and function in a structurally complex set of relationships, and these relationships reveal a multitude of interacting forces that defy a simple cause-effect analysis.

A truly fundamental picture of people and matter as consisting of a continuously moving, dynamic, active process without beginning or ending, in eternal change, represents a basic revolution in our thinking. Inevitably, of course, relativity has revolutionized our ways of talking and writing about the world and the people in it.

The earlier, Aristotelian, view that the world and the things in it, such as desks, books, chairs, and tables, consist of static elements that don't move, has changed to one in which everything and everyone actually consist of continuously moving molecules, but which maintain a form of consistency in terms of whole structures, but which, nonetheless, constantly change in all of their elements.

Many definitions of eternity have been attempted, but none more graphic, perhaps, than that of the preacher who went about it like this: "Brethren and Sisters, if a single sparrow hopped from the Atlantic Ocean to the Pacific Ocean at one hop a day with a single drop of water in its bill, and then hopped back at the same speed and kept this up until all the water in the Atlantic Ocean dropped into the Pacific Ocean, then, we would only arrive at early morning in eternity."

Viewing Reality Differently

Much of the impact of this view of a world in constant change occurs in the way in which we conceive of reality, the manner in which we perceive it, and ways in which we talk about it. This represents the task of trying to describe precisely an object consisting of thousands of incredibly small ping pong balls, all in motion at the same time, and trying to describe the location of every ball while all of them move at indescribable speeds. That task cannot be done accurately. The more complex task involves trying to *predict exactly the location of each and every ball in* **the future**. This constitutes a difficult task because one can locate the position of a ball only when it stops; then, of course, the particles stop moving. But, our earth moves and all the things in it also move; every object and person and event consists of neutrons and protons and molecules and particles in constant movement, often moving in highly unpredictable ways. Sometimes, the products—whole people and machines—look like they move and even seem to move in some predictable manner, but we know that every action has only a degree of probability of moving as we perceive it. We must realize that our observations about the world should result in only tentative conclusions and in terms of the degree of probability of the conclusions representing inaccurate decisions.

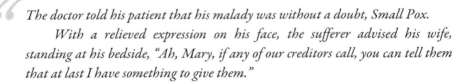

The doctor told his patient that his malady was without a doubt, Small Pox.
With a relieved expression on his face, the sufferer advised his wife, standing at his bedside, "Ah, Mary, if any of our creditors call, you can tell them that at last I have something to give them."

We know that the highly improbable may actually occur—being dealt a perfect hand in cards—but the world of reality consists of a world in process so that our explanations and predictions can be asserted only in terms of probabilities. In other words, what happens on this earth should be described in terms of the probability with which it could happen. Our language permits these kinds of descriptions because it includes symbols that allude to and refer to the probability of things occurring. Something "might" happen or it has the "likelihood" of happening, or it "seemed" to happen that way, or I "thought" it looked like it happened, and so forth.

Our Greatest Illusion: A Reality without Movement

The greatest illusion with which we live as human beings involves the apparent appearance of static, fixed and highly likely happenings. As human beings, the world *looks like* it possesses overwhelming consistencies that allow us to predict precisely what people will do and how they will behave. We talk *as if* the world consisted of "substance" that does not change and that contains something internally static and solid and without movement. As we view or perceive the world, it appears to have considerable stability, jolted only occasionally by the occurrence of some rather improbable events. Our perceptions of and reactions to the world of people, objects, and happenings lead us to create a reality of amazing consistency. That means that our imperfect, insensitive sensing organs encourage us to create a world of motionlessness, fixed, static, immobile events, something quite unlike how the world and people actually function. That, of course, represents just an illusion.

We often fail to realize that an understanding of the world and the people in it mostly comes through our responses to them. We never come into direct contact with the world of people, things and events; we experience only our own personal sensory reactions to the events, things, and people. We do not sense the object itself, but we only feel the responses of our sense organs—touch, see, feel, smell, hear—to the waves of energy that bombard us from the people, objects, and happenings. In other words, we create a picture of the world and the things in it from the light and sound waves, the odors and pressures, and other reactions in the environment. In sum, the process of perception allows us to create what we call information about the world from which we make predictions about happenings, people and events. We should always temper our predictions by our understanding that our perceptions of how people, objects, and events behave may very well provide inaccurate information.

The Processes of Perceiving Reality

As we've noted, individuals create an image of reality by observing or perceiving and "abstracting" from their perceptions an image of what happened. We actually know little about the world and how it operates at a silent level. That is, our senses don't talk to us and explain what happens, we just sense things and construct what we think represents a reasonable prediction about what may happen afterwards. Because we realize that the world functions in constant change, we know that we can make only probable predictions; our perceptions may have errors and very likely the way we talk about our perceptions has errors associated with them.

Alf Morison served as a Veterinarian before the town elected him sheriff, and he continued to ply both trades. One night, shortly after his installation as sheriff, someone knocked on his door. Alf was asleep and his wife raised the upstairs window. "Do you want Alf as Sheriff or as a Vet?" The inquirer said, "I suppose I want a little of both. I want him to help open my bulldog's mouth—he's got a burglar in it."

Levels of Abstraction to Match Worlds of Matter

We noted earlier that our observing and perceiving consists of a process at various levels. We first perceive something, then we find ways to describe our perceptions with symbols such as language and non-verbal signs. After that, we attempt to make sense of what we've described, taking us farther away from our silent perceptions of the reality. Beyond that, we attempt to draw inferences about the quality and veracity of our perceptions, and, eventually, to make generalizations about our perceptions that might help us to predict what will happen in the future. At each level of symbolism, we get farther and farther away from our silent perceptions. We call what we've described as **the process of abstracting** (Korzbyski, 1933, 166-179).

The Structural Differential

The *structural differential* portrays the process of abstracting and provides a visual illustration of the different levels of perceiving and abstracting from our silent perceptions of the world to our conclusions about what we think happened. Perceptions at levels one and two involve non-linguistic events and non-language activities. Bois developed a refined version of Korzybski's differential that distinguishes more clearly among the various levels of description (85).

"Structural Differential"

Level 5 *What I conclude* *about what I say*	Drawing Conclusions from the Interpretations and Creating Generalizations about the Observations of the First-Order Experience	**End Here**
Level 4 *What I say about* *what I said about* *what I saw* *Searle's Person-Related Feature*	Interpretations or Giving Meaning to What was Described or a Third-Order of Experience	

"Structural Differential"

Level 3 *What I say about* *what I see*	Description of What the Observer Observed or the Verbal or Second Order of Experience
Level 2 *What I focus on*	Selection of Details about which the Observer is Concerned or the First-Order Experience

Level 1	The Cosmic Event Itself Consisting of	
What is going on	Trillions of Molecules in Constant Movement	**Start Here**
	but Structured in Forms	

Searle's Intrinsic Feature

Figure 1: Verbal Portrayal of the Process of Abstracting

Let us review each of the levels of abstraction so that we can make distinctions among them later.

Level one represents the sub-microscopic, dynamic world of molecules, atoms, electrons, protons, and quarks that can be known to us only inferentially. Reality consists of relations among the molecules that make up reality, and we call that a *structure*. Structure consists of a complex set of relations among rapidly moving molecules. Korzybski said that *the only content of "knowledge" is structure*. This means that the only things we know consist of perceived connections among elements. Static, immovable, fixed entities do not exist, a reality that we should accept.

Level two represents the nonverbal construction by our nervous systems, reacting to the submicroscopic structures that result in perceptions of objects or our experiences with our surroundings in contrast to what actually exists at the sub-microscopic level. The only knowledge we can create has to do with perceived relationships between and among elements. We understand the world in which we live only through our sensory perceptions of it. One of the major tasks involves making sense of those perceptions. We pick and choose the elements that we assemble to form the picture of a limited totality, object, person, or scene, from the universe of processes that flow incessantly around us. The perceptual level also consists of a non-verbal, silent experience. We attempt to recognize the sensory inputs and give them form. The actual perceptions consist of only silent responses.

Level three represents the first attempt to connect symbols—language—with the nonverbal experience. To give form to the perceptions, we begin the process of attaching symbols to the sensory impressions. Consciousness of abstracting reveals that the only link between the verbal and nonverbal world represents an exclusively structural one. Thinking represents a task of matching the structure of language to the structure of "perceived" reality. This effort to connect words with our perceptions of reality consists of mentally selecting words to name our perceptions. From this point of view, all language consists of names for our sensory perceptions of unspeakable entities on the objective level, be they things or feelings or relations. As we noted earlier, this process leads to two generalizations:

1. Words and the things to which they refer stand independent of each other ["the word is not the thing"], and

2. No object exists in absolute isolation [relations as factors of structure give the sole content of all human knowledge].

Unfortunately, we unconsciously read into the world of reality the structure of the language we use (see Carroll, 1956, 27).

> *Last night a bear slept in its bear skin,*
> *and slept very well I suppose.*
> *But last night I slept in my bare skin,*
> *and I damn near froze.*

Level four represents the descriptive use of language to fill out or elaborate our perceptions of the limitless number of features of the total cosmic event and has to do with "what I say about what I perceived and what I say about what I described."

Level five (and the levels may be limitless, also) concerns the generalizations or conclusions at which we arrive as a result of our descriptions. One way of determining how high on the abstraction ladder we climbed involves figuring out how much guessing a statement requires of a person who wants to have an accurate picture of the situation being described. For example, if I say, "We have a wonderful pet at our place." You ask, "What kind of pet?" and invite me to come down the ladder of abstraction a few rungs. I answer, "We have a dog." You want me to come down lower. "What kind of dog?" you ask. I say, "A Cocker Spaniel." Down more, "What color is it?" I say, "Brown", and on and on until we get to the end of questions or the "silent level." I take you by the hand and show you the dog.

The Frailties of Level Two Perceiving

Unfortunately, we take for granted that the outside world exists actually as we talk about it. We believe implicitly that our mental picture of the world represents reality accurately and every new experience should conform to our pre-established mental picture. Our assumptions, our preconceived notions, particularly those that served us well in the past, act as filters for our abstracting processes. This makes perceiving people, objects, and events a fragile activity.

Accurate Perceptions Lead to Clear-Headedness

Cogency, as well as engaging in cooperative endeavors, depends significantly upon getting clear perceptions of people, objects, and events around us. The term perception refers to a person's experience in sensing, interpreting and comprehending the world in which we live. This makes perception a highly personal and individual act.

> *A hired hand went sparkin' after dinner, and each time, he took a lantern.*
> *The farmer with whom he worked said, "Why the lantern?"*
> *I never went sparkin' with a lantern!"*
> *The hired hand replied, "Yes! And see what you got!"*

As we view the world and the things in it, they appear to have considerable stability, jolting us only occasionally by the occurrence of some rather improbable happenings—a sink-hole opens up under the very house in which we live or a dear friend disappointments us or we perform perfectly on a difficult test. Our perceptions of the world of people, objects, and events lead us to create a reality of amazing consistency. Put another way, our somewhat imperfect and often insensitive sensing organs encourage us to create a world of motionless, fixed, immobile situations, and one not generally representative of life as it actually functions.

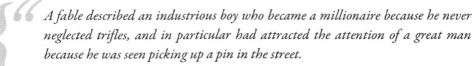

> *A fable described an industrious boy who became a millionaire because he never neglected trifles, and in particular had attracted the attention of a great man because he was seen picking up a pin in the street.*
>
> *Mark Twain was so greatly impressed by this story that when he was a boy looking for a job, he deliberately went to the street in front of an office window and began to pick up pins.*
>
> *After a time, he succeeded in attracting the attention of the man at the desk, who came out and told him, "If you have nothing better to do than pick up pins in the street, you must be an idle and worthless fool."*

We Only Respond to Our Perceptions, Not to Reality

We come to discover reality and the people, objects, and events with which we come in contact only through our personal reactions to our perceptions of them. The key point we want to make states that **we do not respond to people, objects, and events** themselves, but **we respond only to our perceptions of those** people, objects and events. Thus, we respond to our sense organs and to the waves of energy that bombard us from the objects: to the light and sound waves, for example. As I write this sentence, I sense some object flying past my computer screen. I don't respond to the fly directly, but I get a sense of sight and sound and movement and I suspect that something I call a fly intrudes on my concentration. So far I ignore it, but gradually, I experience those sensations more intently and decide that I don't want it to occupy some of my space, so I reach for my fly swatter.

> *A visitor to the home of Mark Twain remarked upon the great number of books, many of which lay around in piles without adequate provision for shelving them. "You see," Twain explained, "I find it very difficult to borrow shelves."*

What happens when we perceive something visually, for example? In somewhat oversimplified terms, at least two things occur. First, light rays reflect from the person, object, or event being observed and focus on the retina or back wall of the eye. Second, the rays transform into electrical impulses that the optical nerve transmits to the brain. This process involves certain electro-chemical responses that stimulate areas in the cerebral cortex and result in the act of "seeing." The procedures seem quite similar for each of the other human senses. When you say, "I see a face," you actually mean, "I visually perceive the face." Living in a world that keeps moving and changing continuously, we can argue that your precise location and sensory system may also change so that you cannot duplicate the same scene. In addition, what you perceive can't duplicate what others perceive and no one else can duplicate your perceptions.

Certainly, with appropriate safeguards and provisions for the improbable, some sense of accuracy can evolve from our visual perceptions, and, of course, with the other senses as well. Two basic sources appear to influence our perceptions:

1. A person's **peculiar physiological makeup** that allows for certain physical structures to induce illusions of the existence of certain realities when those realities simply do not exist.

2. An unsorted stock of **memories, interpretations, and prejudices** that have accumulated within us during the course of our lives that induce unusual and inaccurate interpretations of what we think we perceive.

Consequently, what we actually react to may have features considerably different from what we think we perceive. For example, when an object seems to increase in size on the retina of our eyes, we interpret this not as an increase in size, but rather as movement toward us. Boulding (1956) explained the experience in this way: "We only get along in the world because we consistently and persistently disbelieve the plain evidence of our senses" (p. 14). In addition, we tend to convert only a small portion of the raw sensory data we pick up from our perceptions into "information" or mental images, ideas, and reactions. Thus, we assume that what we talk about and write about represents only a very small part of all that appears to occur inside of us as well as out there in the external world. And, of course, we may not actually perceive even a very small portion accurately.

Perceptions Susceptible to Tricks

We have a couple of explanations for these inaccuracies. In the first place, because of human physiological limitations, we may trick the normal eye and brain into seeing things that exist differently from how they appear. Books of optical illusions have been published by Al Seckel (2006) and by Keith Kay and five other authors (2003). They explain that optical illusions play tricks on our eyes and baffle our perceptions. Depending on the light and angle of sight or the way one draws an image, we may see things that just do not exist. Our eyes gather impressions, but the brain interprets the perceptions and tries to make sense out of what the eyes see. If our eyes appear to see something that the brain can't immediately understand, it corrects the image so that the perception makes sense.

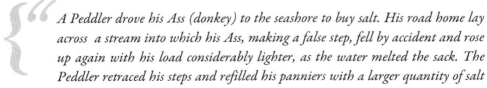

A Peddler drove his Ass (donkey) to the seashore to buy salt. His road home lay across a stream into which his Ass, making a false step, fell by accident and rose up again with his load considerably lighter, as the water melted the sack. The Peddler retraced his steps and refilled his panniers with a larger quantity of salt

than before. When he came again to the stream, the Ass fell down on purpose in the same spot, and, regaining his feet with the weight of his load much diminished, prayed triumphantly as if he had obtained what he desired.

The Peddler saw through his trick and drove him for the third time to the coast, where he bought a cargo of sponges instead of salt. The Ass, again playing the fool, fell down on purpose when he reached the stream, but the sponges became swollen with water, greatly increasing his load. And thus his trick recoiled on him, for he now carried on his back a double burden.

Seckel explains, however, that the power of some illusions trick you to the extent that even though you "know" we devised a trick, you cannot recognize the trick. A key principle about perceptions of reality says that Seeing is NOT believing, meaning that what you see may not exist and you should not necessarily believe it just because you think you saw something. This inability to see things as they actually exist and to describe the world of reality precisely, just making some reasonable predictions about the character of the world and the people, objects and events that occur in it, seems about the best we can do.

Believing IS Seeing

Although we focused on the effects of prior experience and physiological conditions on what we perceive and say about reality, we must also realize that what we say also influences our perceptions and our views of reality. This tends to occur as a result of the *Mind-Set* that we bring to our perceptions. Our previous life experiences and previous perceptions and expectations bear heavily on our current perceptions. A simple experiment will demonstrate how what we call something affects what we see in the situation. Look at the drawing below without assuming that you see anything but a set of lines.

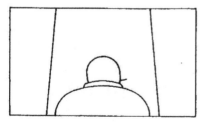

Now, believe that the drawing represents (1) a cooking utensil. What do you see? Write down the name of the utensil and briefly explain how you use it.

Now look at the drawing and think of it as (2) a weapon of war. What do you see? Write down the name of the weapon and briefly explain how you use it.

Now look at the drawing and think of it as (3) a sketch of a particular person. Who do you see? Write down the name of the specific person represented by the drawing.

Now look at the drawing and think of it as representing (4) an animal. What do you see? Write down the name of the animal and briefly explain what actions you see the animal doing.

Let us analyze your responses in the sequence of believing-seeing. In the first perception, did you see the drawing representing something like *a tea kettle*? In the second perception, did you see the drawing representing *a tank*? In the third perception did you see the specific person whom we recognize as *Winston Churchill*, the imposing British statesman? In the fourth perception, did you see the *first-place racehorse* from the perspective of the second-place jockey?

Did your perceptions of what the drawing represented change four times; did you accurately predict that what you thought or believed in advance affected what you saw in the drawing? Did our labeling the figure in the drawing in advance influence what you saw afterwards? The significance of this tendency cannot receive too much emphasis. When you heard the label, did you immediately look for that particular person, object or event in the drawing? Think of this sequence: We gave you a label—*cooking utensil*, you looked for an object in that category that you could name. When you heard the category *weapon of war*, you looked for an object in a different category that you could name; when you heard the category *animal*, you looked for an object in a different category. You may have taken more time to visualize in your mind an animal and you may have delayed seeing a race horse until someone described it for you, especially the *jockey*.

Nevertheless, the tendency—even the absolute necessity—to attach names and labels to the results of your perceptions facilitates and even dictates what you purport to *know* about the world around you. In order to change your perceptions of that single drawing to see four different *realities* depends on labeling each one. When you label a person, you see the person that way. When you label a woman *beautiful*, regardless of her physical attributes, you see her as consistent with the label. Believing is seeing leads strongly to the *Is of Identity* and the *Is of Predication*.

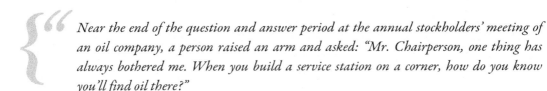

Near the end of the question and answer period at the annual stockholders' meeting of an oil company, a person raised an arm and asked: "Mr. Chairperson, one thing has always bothered me. When you build a service station on a corner, how do you know you'll find oil there?"

Your best defense against engaging in categorizing and projecting attributes on people, objects, and events takes the form of resisting to use any form of *the verb To Be*; without the verb of existence or projection, you'll feel compelled to re-evaluate your perceptions and guard against responding to the labels, as you did in naming the perceptions in advance in our little experiment, and seek to describe your perceptions more directly.

Tendencies toward Elementalism

You should also have a greater awareness of the tendency to divide up the indivisible in reality using labels. You wrote Race Horse or *racehorse*, depending on your view of the animal perceived. Maybe we should have said *cookingutensil* rather than Cooking Utensil. Maybe we should write *believingseeing* or *thinkingbelieving* rather than try to divide two intertwined perceptual actions.

Verbal Ineptitudes

We lack certainty of what we sense and we lack certainty that we have the ability to create accurate information, and we lack certainty that our predictions and statements sound infallible. Beyond that, we seem totally unaware of the dissimilarity between the structure of the language we use and the structure of the real world. The differences may lead to misevaluations and subsequent maladjustments (Johnson, 1946; Murray and Barbour, 1973). In paraphrasing Wendell Johnson, we summarize the potentially widespread consequences of language-behavior problems:

We may observe the verbal ineptitude of people in quandaries by the extremes of verbal output; in the rigidity of evaluations; in dead-level abstracting; in elementalistic responses and absolutism; and in either-or responses to situations. We may also observe verbal ineptitude by the meaningless and mis-directive character of many of the questions which people persistently ask—or which they unreflectively attempt to answer. Johnson evokes some solace when he asserts that

> *With a fair amount of practice, one can become reasonably skilled in observing these characteristics of language behavior in oneself and in others. The ability to recognize them gives one a measure of control over them, and a degree of insight into the basic mechanisms of adequate evaluation. It enables one to recognize a fool—and to avoid being one—a bit more readily than would otherwise [thought] possible (293).*

Preliminary Conclusions about Abstracting

From the analysis of the relationship of our perceptions to the world of constantly moving and changing elements, we can suggest some possible implications. We conclude that:

1. We can know reality--people, objects, and events--only through our sensory reactions to them, and then not directly, only as responses filtered through our nervous systems.
2. People, objects, and happenings may trigger our sensory receptors, but we still may not perceive reality because we have not focused on the sensation and because perceptual illusions occur as a result of perceptual limitations.
3. Even happenings that we do observe stand a risk of having certain aspects omitted or change or added so that what we perceive rarely corresponds exactly with the reality observed; most of our perceptions represent only approximations of the actual world in which we live.
4. We tend to perceive reality in terms of our past experiences, our assumptions, and our intentions, so that we focus on what we want or what we seem capable of perceiving.
5. No two people perceive the world in identical ways because our perceptions come from highly individual and personal experiences, assumptions, and intentions. Some perceptions provide good approximations because the two people share similar experiences, assumptions, and intentions.

6. *Meanings* assigned to people, objects, and events differ, also, due to those differences in perceptions; since we behave pretty much consistent with our perceptions and assigned meanings, our behavior also differs.

7. Perceptions tend to persist unless we find that the actions based on those perceptions experience frustration or negation. We change our actions because we discover that our intentions cannot be achieved, not because someone tells us that we have wrong perceptions or intentions.

8. Perceptions often result from the language patterns and communicative habits that we develop early in life. Stability, rigidity, standardization, and resistance to change tend to characterize our behaviors, which depend in no small part on the categories created by our language. In brief, perceptions influence our language patterns, and our language patterns influence our perceptions.

Sometimes and Perhaps

We live in a reality of *sometimes and perhaps* where we had hoped to live *with always and certainty*. Having stated that we can never really describe reality precisely, does that mean that we should give up trying, that we should ignore reality? Decidedly not! We have no choice. Reality exists; it surrounds us. However, reality exists in ways that we often have difficulty comprehending; nevertheless, much of our understanding of people, objects, and events consists in giving every little part a category and a name. For most practical purposes, the shape and qualities of the elements of reality come from our projections and classifications of them by the language we use to describe them.

> *The Texan seemed impressed by the wonders of Australia until a kangaroo hopped by. "Ah'll grant you one thing," he said to the Aussie. "Your grasshoppers are bigger than ours.*

Thus, our primary goals involve developing ways to evaluate our perceptions and the way we talk about them so as to provide the most accurate, the most meaningful ways of thinking about and talking about and responding to the realities with which we deal during our lives on this earth. The next issue has to do with how we achieve that goal (Paraphrased from Johnson, 1946, 185-189).

Part IV: How?

How We Make Corrections to Avoid Appearing Foolish!

Bois (1978) explains that as we continue to progress in maintaining well-adjusted and wise versus foolish ways of behaving, "more and more indicators of safe or dangerous semantic functioning can be observed by the layperson. They require no laboratory apparatus or psychological testing devices. They fit within the observable range of what we say, what we do, how we say it, and how we do it. They can be measured on a qualitative scale, from danger to safety . . ." (p. 279).

> *Is sloppiness in speech caused by ignorance or apathy?*
> *I don't know and I don't care.*

A Diagnostic Look at Danger Signals and Safety Measures

Below we list some indicators of danger in language usage and their safety counterparts so you can use language and non-language behaviors that build powerful and well-adjusted lives.

Danger Indicators	Safety Measures
1. Use of absolute terms, generalizations, and statements that imply "allness" and high order abstractions.	Use descriptive terms that employ specific who, where, what, when, and how and avoid higher order abstractions. Keep absolute, sweeping, and general terms to less than 15% of your language.
2. Use of judgment and loaded terms or disapproval.	Use of neutral terms and terms that imply approval that are as free as possible from bias or slant. Avoid terms such as "you should," "you must," "the only thing to do is . . . ."
3. Use of either-or arguments, passing from one alternative to its extreme opposite while describing things in terms of "black and white."	Speak in terms of more-or-less, give consideration to degrees and shades of meaning; avoid talking in terms of opposites without any gray shading in between.

Danger Indicators	Safety Measures
4. Speaking of the present situation as another one; as this person just like so and so; and this problem just like one earlier.	Differentiate carefully between "just like" this problem and one solved earlier. Individuals who boast of having "experience" solving problems, often assume that their earlier problems look like the present ones.
5. Confuse "facts" that can be verified by anyone with interpretations, opinions, and judgments that are exclusively their own.	Distinguish carefully between what is actually going on and what you feel or think is going on. This means to avoid confusing second-order inferences with first-order facts.
6. Ramble from one subject to another.	Keep talking on the subject under discussion.
7. Constantly quote "authorities" to uphold their own points of view.	Evaluate situations on their own merits.
8. Quibble on the "dictionary" meaning of words.	Use words as simply representations of what we're referring to.
9. Talk too fast and too loud to make a point.	Talk calmly and with deliberation.
10. Interrupt others by starting to talk before they have finished a thought and contradict what was said.	Listen with genuine interest and wait for a turn to speak, even allowing some silence in order to understand what a person says with a "ya-but" or a well-a-but". Allow a second or two to elapse between the last words you hear and your response.
11. When talking, keep muscles tense, move in jerks, and fidget, and twitch.	Relax, remain calm and quiet, and delay your reactions to what was said until you feel calm.
12. Ask rhetorical, self-answering questions, or tricky questions.	Ask matter-of-fact questions that invite information or opinions for answers, and avoid questions that involve puzzles.
13. Take yourself too seriously.	Keep a sense of humor.

The Basic Principles of Well-Adjusted Language Use

Bourland (1996) provides us with an E-Prime version of the three basic principles of language use to guide us in developing counter-actions so as move closer to communicating as well-adjusted adults. We state each new E-Prime definition just below the title of each one.

The Principle of Non-Identity

Non-Identity: A "map" or word belongs to a level of abstraction different from that of the "territory" or aspect of reality it purports to represent.

Use E-Prime Language to Correct Identity Problems

Since the time we recognized the devastating consequences of the Is of Identity and Predication, David Bourland, a student of language usage, introduced a method for removing some of the inaccuracies from our language. He called it "E-Prime Language," which consists of eliminating all forms of the *verb to be* from our thinking, speaking, and writing, including, **am, be, being, been, is, are, isn't, it's, was, were, wasn't, weren't, you're, we're, they're, there's, here's, where's, how's, what's, and who's,** from our vocabulary.

E-Prime language also removes the passive voice from statements, a distinct benefit toward achieving accuracy in language. For example, the statement: "The movie was good," a passive tense, could find expression in a different form. As structured, the statement has no agent. A better statement might read: "I liked the movie", since the revised statement communicates the subjective nature of the speaker's experience, rather than implying a static goodness to the movie. "Goodness" cannot exist in the movie. "Goodness" simply represents your judgment of the quality of the movie. Your statement about the movie should indicate that you made the judgment about it.

Now, to experience E-Prime language, rewrite some of these classic but slightly maladjusted statements to reflect a more accurate expression. For example, take Hamlet's familiar utterance, "To be or not to be, that is the question." How about restating it to ask, "I ask the question, should I live or should I die?" Now, study the following restatements of other classic utterances:

Roses are red, violets are blue. Honey is sweet. And so are you.
The original structure represents a predication error: you project red onto a flower, sweet onto honey, and sweetness onto some person. Try the following restatement:
   Roses look red; violets look blue; honey pleases me, and so do you.
This restatement represents a literal translation, which avoids predication, and the speaker making a false or maladjusted statement.

Roses look red, violets look blue, and honey tastes sweet, as sweet as you.
This restatement also represents a literal translation, but implies an "**are**" ending.
   Roses seem red, violets seem blue. I like honey, and I like you too.
This statement expresses meaning directly, expresses the speaker's personal feelings, and represents an accurate statement of reality.

If you find it difficult to write or speak in E-Prime language, refer to your basic "silent level" experience and describe the actual event, such as expressed in the following restatements:

Statement	*Restatement for Accuracy at a First Order*
Science and Sanity is a great book!	*I really enjoyed reading Science and Sanity.*
The food at KFC is good.	*I like the taste of KFC food.*

Joan is smart.   *Joan makes $500,000 a year.*

Clive is smart.   *Clive scored 160 on an IQ test.*

Dave is a doctor.   *Dave practices medicine.*

All of these restatements translate inaccurate statements into accurate ones and reduce the likelihood that you might have a tendency to make a damn fool of yourself. Now, Re-write the following statements into E-Prime language.

1. *Risa is a teacher.*_____

2. *Joe is a car mechanic.*_____

3. *Is Lisa there?*_____

4. *What is your name?*_____

5. *How are you?*_____

6. *It was done.*_____

7. *Jack was blessed.*_____

8. *The experiment was conducted by Mike.* _____

9. *Waiting is the right thing to do.* _____

10. *People from New Jersey are weird.* _____

11. *Politicians are crooked.* _____

12. *People over thirty are out of it.* _____

13. *Obedience to authority is the most important virtue a child can learn.*

    _____

14. *What is correct English?* _____

15. *You are not trying hard enough.* _____

16. *I am a gloomy person.* _____

17. *Henry is an ugly person.*+ _____

18. *He is a tough professor._* _____

19. *What is correct English?* _____

20. *The car is magenta.* _____

Let us now chat about the second principle leading to well-adjusted language behavior.

The Principle of Non-Allness

Non-Allness: A "map" or word does not contain all of the structural characteristics of the "territory" or reality it purports to represent.

Avoid Allness Statements: Therapy for All-Inclusive Generalizations. Even with the most exhaustive analysis that the minds and methods of contemporary humankind can apply to our earthly realities—people, objects, and events—a complete description and prediction will not occur. We possess too many limitation in our abilities to describe everything in, about, and around the earth, making it impossible to comprehend and communicate every that seems applicable and true about all of it.

In support of that conclusion, we need only remind ourselves that language at best stands at least once removed from that to which it refers, that words as such only represent the perceptions we experience about the total reality of where we live. Moreover, when we try to describe something, we use words that focus on certain details while ignoring others. As a matter of fact, whenever we talk, write, listen, read, or simply observe something, we naturally and necessarily engage in abstracting; and, when we abstract, we focus on only limited facets of any particular person, object, or happening. Thus, it makes sense to concur with the claim that to know everything and to explain everything absolutely just cannot occur; to describe everything about even a single object, person, or event resembles an impossible task. Nevertheless, on occasion and more often than we should to stay healthy, we behave **AS IF** we have the capability to say everything about what we think we see in the world. With our special command of language, we think we have the ability and talent to "know it all," which leads to the use of an inordinately large number of **Know It All** statements. We call people who engage in allness or know it all statements as **Closed Minded** or people who talk as if they could know absolutely everything about something and employ language that presumes to describe that something completely and accurately.

The Fox and the Goat

> *A fox one day fell into a deep well and could find no means of escape. A goat, overcome with thirst, came to the same well, and seeing the fox, inquired if the water was good. Concealing his sad plight under a merry guise, the fox indulged in a lavish praise of the water, saying it was excellent beyond measure, and encouraging him to descend.*
>
> *The goat, mindful only of his thirst, thoughtlessly jumped down, but just as he drank, the fox informed him of the difficulty they were both in and suggested a scheme for their common escape.*
>
> *"If," said he, "you will place your forefeet upon the wall and bend your head, I will run up your back and escape, and will help you out afterwards."*
>
> *The goat readily assented and the fox leaped upon his back. Steadying himself with the goat's horns, he safely reached the mouth of the well and made*

off as fast as he could.

When the goat upbraided him for breaking his promise, he turned around and cried out, "You foolish old fellow! If you had as many brains in your head as you have hairs in your beard, you would never have gone down before you had inspected the way up, nor have exposed yourself to dangers from which you had no means of escape."

This tendency toward uttering know-it-all statements and acting as if you know it all and demonstrate close-mindedness poses one of the major obstacles to productive interpersonal interaction. We ought to deal with others with open hearts and open minds, but too often we speak with **tones** of finality and punctuate the end of an utterance so as to give the unmistakable impression that we possess the right, correct, exact, and unalterable conclusion. At such moments, we function deliberately or unintentionally with closed minds.

Do you occasionally notice that you say, "That's not right!" "I know what I'm talking about!" "Let me tell you how things really are!" "This is so simple that even you can understand it!" Or "the correct idea is stated like this!" Utterances of this tenor, especially when expressed in a tone of unwavering "self-rightness" and "determination" show symptoms of close-mindedness and represent narrow, dogmatic, and rigid language malfunctioning. The reduction of this kind of "allness-know it all" language patterns represents one of the most important tasks in which you can engage to keep the door of your mind open for new information and to maintain positive relationships with others.

> *A mountain was once greatly agitated.*
> *Loud groans and noises were heard, and crowds of people*
> *Came from all parts to see what was the matter.*
> *While they were assembled in anxious expectation of some*
> *Terrible calamity, out came a mouse.*
> *Moral: Don't make much ado about nothing.*

Beware of Tone or Tonicity

The tone of something has to do with a manner of speaking or writing that shows a particular attitude on the part of the speaker or writer. Tones achieve certain effects and create specific moods. Studies of nonverbal behavior indicate that we use many different languages, not just a language, such as English. Although we may all speak so-called English, we use different tones that create different forms of English. For example, we have a language for formal settings and a language for football games. One "language" doesn't fit all occasions. To discover the meaning of different tones, engage in the following exercises:

Exercise 1: Reading a Fable

Read the fable about a rabbit who boasted too much, emphasizing the tones of voice of the different descriptive terms and phrases highlighted.

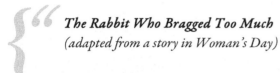

The Rabbit Who Bragged Too Much
(adapted from a story in Woman's Day)

A family of rabbits lived in a **thick** part of a wooded area. Most of the time they seemed **happy** until one of the younger ones called **Flappy** made life **miserable** for all of the family. If you know any rabbits **personally**, you realize that they need two things to get along well in the world. They need to **run** very fast and they need to **hear** very well. Maybe you've noticed that their **strong** back legs allow them to jump and run away from hawks and especially **dogs**. Their **long** ears aid them to hear anything that comes to **chase** them, so they usually get a head start on getting away from **trouble**.

Flappy ran fast **alright**. Everyone knew that. They could see it for themselves. However, Flappy **bragged** and **boasted** about how fast he could run until it made the long ears of the whole family **ache**. He **puffed** himself up and went on for **hours** about how he **tricked** an old farmer into **falling** over a wheel barrow in **his own** lettuce patch trying to catch Flappy. He **bragged on and on** that no dog could catch him. Listening to him created a bad pain in everyone's ears. Flappy exhibited so much **confidence** in his abilities that he didn't **even bother** to carry his ears up high so he could hear things coming. He just let his ears **droop down**, which led to calling him Flappy.

One day while he **nibbled** on a carrot that he **stole** from the old farmer, something suddenly gave his cotton tail a **sharp** tug. **"Ouch,"** he said, and turned to **stare** into the face of a dog he didn't recognize. The dog's long **skinny legs** looked something like a **half-twisted** rope. However, the dog showed his **sharp,** white teeth in a **grin** and said, "I hear **you brag** a lot about how fast you can run. Well, **get going** before I **shred** you into stew meat. On your **mark**, get set, **GO!**"

Flappy took **three big hops** and stretched out for the long run. He looked back and the **mangy** dog just sat there waiting to give him a **long** head start. Then, all of a sudden, **SWOOSH**, the dog **shot** past him like a **raging** bullet. Before you could say **Jack Rabbit**, the dog caught up with Flappy. "I **thought** you told everyone you could **run fast**," the dog **sneered** and showed his teeth again. Flappy took a **deep** breath and **sprang** out with every bit of energy he possessed. Old Mangy ran circles around Flappy until **poor** old Flappy just couldn't skip or jump another **hop**. Old Mangy gave Flappy's tail another **jerk** and **laughed** out loud and said, "Now **stay out** of the Farmer's vegetable garden and go home and tell your family that you met a **dog** who could **really run**." Flappy **sauntered** home and that night he just **listened** to what the others said

*about their days, and he **stopped** bragging and boasting and **listened very well**
ever after.*

What difference did emphasizing particular words make to your response to the story? What kind of **tone** did those emphases create in the story? Did the story seem to take on a different meaning with the emphasized words? Did emphasizing different words create any particular mood in the story?

From this experience, you should discover that the tone in which you express a word has an effect on the meanings created by those listening to the story.

Exercise 2: Using Tonicity in Describing a Picture to Illustrate Intensionality

Select a picture that shows several characters doing one or two tasks, such as people working or just talking to one another. Describe the picture using a different tone of voice for each character in the picture. Describe what the characters say, how they act, and how they sound. Poets use this feature of language to consciously create a mood or feeling. Certain words have a unique function in eliciting feelings and creating moods. From this experience, you may demonstrate for yourself and for others how tonicity affects the meaning of occurrences viewed in the picture. Tonicity may elicit intense reactions at times.

Reactions to tonicity tend to occur because of the tendency of people to respond to words rather than to the events they represent. We often react to the words themselves, without any actual events taking place. This represents the principle of *Identify*. We can't express too strongly the importance of have a strong awareness of the possibility of responding to words only, without any presence of a reality. The strength of the tone associated with certain words may possibly lead to an intensional orientation and maladjusted reactions.

Exercise 3: Tonicity in Party Invitations

Prepare three different invitations to parties you and your spouse, partner or friend plan to give for a group in your community. Invite people with whom you have experience and feel friendly toward. For the first invitation use very formal language; for the second, write in very casual and informal language; for the third invitation, use slang and poor grammar.

Use these questions to analyze reactions to the three different invitations:

1. Do the invitations suggest differences . . .

a. about those doing the inviting?

b. in attire worn to the different parties?

c. in the types of "gifts" to be taken?

d. in where the party might be held?

e. in the type of food served?

2. Which words in the invitations set the tone?

Exercise 4. Writing Stories with the Same Plot but Different Word-Tones

Provide a list of words that suggest different tones, such as

Obese	*vs*	*Fat*
Walk	*vs*	*Stomp*
Fly	*vs*	*Flit*
Incident	*vs*	*Affair*
Dine	*vs*	*Eat*
Hungry	*vs*	*Starved*

Write two stories with the same plot. In one story use the more formal type of words and in the other, use the more informal words. You should discover that the "tone" of the story changes according to the type of words used.

Allness statements get all tangled up with our orientations toward language use. We shall now review the key differences between a desirable Extensional orientation and an undesirable Intensional orientation.

Differences between Intensional and Extensional Orientations

The terms *extension* and *intension* express a special meaning for people engaged in the study of language usage. To adopt an *intensional* orientation toward language and behavior individuals largely disregard observations of the world and react to the language statements.

Intensional Orientation

An intensional orientation to the relationship of language and behavior means that a person pays **more attention to words written or said about** a person, object or event **than to the person, object or event itself**. Several research studies reveal that when individuals evaluated the quality of products, they paid more attention to advertising copy than to the products themselves. Advertisers often depend on people taking an intensional approach to their products and have copy writers provide glowing descriptions. Thus, intensionally-oriented customers could just read the copy and make judgments about the products without actually looking at the products themselves.

Another feature of an intensional orientation concerns **how uncritically people react to words they hear or read**. This means that people may react to the tone associated with words themselves rather than to the symbolic role of words to represent something else. This kind of response occurs when someone describes a hay stack and the allergies that occur with the dust stirred up and you sneeze as a result. Another instance of an intensional orientation occurred when a woman said that she had an allergy to cats and when reading a passage from a book about a person who had a fondness for cats, she sneezed and suffered other symptoms of allergies to fur. Many other psychosomatic illnesses develop as a result of an intensional orientation to words.

Extensional Orientation

An extensional orientation means that a person seeks to observe what really happens before making judgments about the happening. They do not rely just on words and statements, but they examine the actual event if at all possible.

Extensionally-oriented individuals seek answers to what, why, and who of a situation before drawing conclusions about it. They inquire, behave with curiosity, and attempt to determine what actually happened. They behave more like investigative reporters than opinion columnists. An extensional orientation involves, as often as possible, actually pointing to the experience or happening under consideration rather than talking about it. Strictly speaking, extensionality functions entirely at the nonverbal level in that, as often as possible, describe in sufficient detail so as to verbally point to an exact example of the situation. Operational definitions, as discussed earlier, represent extensional orientations involving the use of words. A summary statement of extensionalism says that the adequate evaluation of a situation depends on how well one's assumptions measure up against actual nonverbal experience and the "facts" of the situation.

Consistently Use Extensional Language Devices

Korzybski (1933, 1948) provided a series of **extensional devices**, the uses of which automatically bring about an orientation in conformity with the latest scientific discoveries about reality. These devises help increase one's "consciousness of abstracting" and free you from archaic limitations inherent in "standard" English. The devices often go by the designation of "structural expedients." The devices simply allow you to provide descriptions that recognize the process nature of the world and our inability to predict events accurately.

Indexes: Using indexes-- republican 1, republican 2, republican 3--reminds us that individuals exhibit differences as well as similarities with others of the same name, place, etc. A word lumps together unique individuals under a common name. Names give a false impression of identity (sameness). This impression, when translated into behavior, results in semantic reactions to all individuals to whom the same name can be given, etc.

Dates: Adding a date to categories such as people--Pace 1950, Pace 1960, Pace 1970, Pace 1980, Pace 2007--reminds us that the same person or object responds differently at different times and in different environments.

This device takes into account the fact that an object or person with the same name varies over time. The habit of placing dates on the names of persons, objects, and events makes it difficult to respond to them as if they had not changed over time.

Etc. or Etcetera: The use of both vocal and verbal *etc's* at the end of most statements reminds us that language maps (words) do not represent all the attributes of a territory (person, object, event), and that no statements about a territory cover everything about any topic, etc. This device reminds us of the many factors in a process that one can never fully know or perceive and facilitates flexibility and a greater degree of conditionality in our semantic reactions. This device leads away from dogmatism, absolutism, and close-mindedness, etc.

Quotes: Putting quotation marks around multiordinal terms such as "love," "happy," "management," "prominent," and "facts" alerts others to the possibility that many different meanings from what seems apparent may exist in the minds of others.

This device reminds us that many terms represent different levels of abstraction and multiordinality and have special, personal meanings. Such terms may not represent the events in the way others think.

Hyphens: Expressions such as time-space, psycho-logic, socio-cultural, bio-physical sharpen your awareness of the interrelatedness of objects, events, and subject matters when traditional language treats them as unrelated.

This hyphen device reminds us that traditional language verbally separates many things that do not exist separately in reality, called **elementalism**. A single word tends to imply unjustified "unity" and obscures inter-acting complexities.

Plurals: potentialities, experiences, manuals, books, strategies, and selves represent pluralities in reality. If we write and speak more in plurals, we reflect the multidimensionality of life and existence. Plurals also allow you to avoid inaccuracies when referring to multiple genders.

This device reminds us that existence consists of many dimensions and that people themselves consist of multiple perspectives.

Verbal Qualifiers: "As far as I know", "up to a point", "from where I stood" represent expressions that limit, restrict, circumscribe, temper, modify, modulate, and narrow the conditions under which we observe, perceive, and assess situations, events, people, and objects to the precise moment at which the observations, etc. occurred. Such phrases tend to sharpen our senses and language and make our statements more accurate. This device reminds us that our observations may create our own facts and that our observations represent a combination of what occurs inside of us and what happens outside of us.

The Principle of Awareness of Self-Reflexiveness

Meta-Language: A "map" or word self-reflectively contains a "map" or description of a higher order which shows the relation between the "territory" or reality represented in some detail to the surrounding "territory" or reality.

The uses of Meta-Language

This principle expresses the fundamental notion that "seeing" something consists of a process that selects some details and leaves out others details. We call this "abstracting." One can never say all about anything, just as one can never observe all of anything. Non-allness provides us with greater assurance that we should behave as if we know that our knowledge and our statements cannot describe an event completely.

Show an Awareness of Different Levels of Abstraction

To ensure reliability in our language use, we need to build into it forms of specificity. We need an awareness and consciousness of using language that moves from "higher orders" to "lower orders" or general to particular. Misunderstandings may occur until we move from higher levels of abstraction to lower levels, which results in the process of giving examples.

Exercise 1: Pictures of Levels of Abstractions

For example, you may recognize different levels of abstracting by looking at pictures that go from the abstract to the specific, such as pictures of all types of animals (abstract) to pictures of pet animals only (specific); pictures of small animals (abstract) to a pictures of a small dog (specific); pictures of all types of food (abstract) to pictures of fruits only; pictures of several yellow fruits (abstract) to a picture of a lemon (specific).

Exercise 2: Words that Include More or Less of Things

Circle the word that covers MORE things.

insects	*or*	*animals*
flowers	*or*	*roses*
George	*or*	*child*
animal	*or*	*dog*
clothes	*or*	*dress*
fruit	*or*	*food*

Write out concrete examples of each of the following abstract terms:

Honesty

Patriotism

Courage

Gentleness

Friendliness

Loyalty

Patience

Anger

Arrange the following words in terms of levels of abstraction by placing a (1), (2), (3), and (4) in the space next to the vertical list of words with (4) representing the highest level of abstraction and (1) the lowest, most concrete level of abstraction:

Pet _____	*School* _____	*Principal* _____
St Bernard _____	*Structure* _____	*Person* _____
Animal _____	*Wood Elementary* _____	*Man* _____

Dog _____   Brown Building _____   Mr. Jones _____

    Write __A__ before any abstract word and __C__ before any concrete word:
| | |
_____ 1. Wheel   _____ 4. Glasses   _____ 7. heroism

_____ 2. Loveliness   _____ 5.Ronald Reagan   _____ 8. Hercules

_____ 3. Rose   _____ 6. Patriotism   _____ 9. Kindness

After each of the words below, write one other more concrete word:

1. mammal _____   4. job _____   7. cake _____

2. plant _____   5. Scientist _____ 8. fruit _____

3. story _____   6. Wood _____   9. Medicine _____

    Complete each sentence by underling the most specific descriptive word:

1.   My father works as a [specialist, professional, surgeon, doctor].

2.   Sally likes to read [a novel, a book, literature, Robin Hood].

3.   Our family lived in [Germany, the Eastern Hemisphere, Europe, Frankfurt]

4.   I call Scottie my [pet, animal, dog, terrier]

5.   Class members use [a pen, a ball point, a writing instrument, a Papermate]

6.   The recipe called for [sugar, a sweetener, an ingredient, 4 X sugar].

    In the space beneath each sentence, arrange all of the choices according to the levels of abstraction from most general to most specific.

Summary

In this Part we attempted to make some comments about the pragmatics of language and a contemporary approach to thought, language, and behavior. We described the main themes of the field in which reality, perceptions, and symbols merge--communication. Our discussion distinguished among people as time-binders, animals as space-binders, and plants as chemical-binders. A number of critical principles emerged, including consciousness of abstracting and the Structural Differential, and perceptual processes. We discussed some principles governing the real world in which we live and the frailties of trying to perceive everything and talk as if we could say everything about anything. We talked about self-reflectiveness and multiordinality, frozen evaluations, polarizations, and disqualifying personalizations. We talked about E-Prime language and extensional language devices.

Part V: Where?

Where Do We find Out How We Did?

Explanation of Purpose of Measurement

For the most part, our concerns here have to do with how well you have acquired knowledge. As a multiordinal term, we need to talk about the specific meanings which we tend to use in this context. To know something, tends to mean that you have the ability to *recognize* the features or elements of something and the similarities and differences among the elements, and to recognize how similar a situation seems to one experienced previously; to have an awareness of the truth or factuality of a statement; to recall statements; to break information into parts or analyze something; to bring together unrelated parts; to interpret or bring meaning to something; and to determine how well something works.

Philosophically, we assume that we can only sample or select a few items to represent responses from a much larger universe. We assume that you recognize that by responding to a few items, you simply predict that you know something about the larger universe. We hope that you may get some sense of the broad scope of the topics addressed in this book by responding to a limited number of statements, exercises, and problems.

Measurements of Your Understanding about the Readings

Concept Identification

Instructions: Identify the concept by name and the philosopher associated with it.

1. All things have a nature of their own;   **Name**   **Philosopher**
   a person is a person.   _____ _____
2. A set of fundamental units from which you can forecast
   the fate of the universe--its molecules and its people, and
   its nations from now into eternity.   _____ _____
3. A fact and an observer do not exist separately, but
   joining the two has occurred; it replaces the idea of
   the inevitable effect by the probable trend. _____ _____

Instructions: Name the concept.   **Concept**

4. The consistently predictable measured by how much one can
    predict on the basis of the assertion; we recognize
    "Red" as a wavelength of about one three-hundred
    thousandth of an inch. _____

5. A method shared by the whole society consciously and at one time
    so that the society sees it as communicable and systematic. _____

6. The view that a desk, a book, and a blackboard actually consist
    of continuously moving molecules that maintain a
    constancy in terms of a whole._____

7. A neural process involving the perceptual selecting
    and omitting of details._____

8. When, without any change in its dictionary meaning, a word
    used in the same sentence or context refers to different
    orders of abstraction._____

9. We say that we moved from the nonverbal reality to what we
    pay attention to and our personal concerns._____

10. At times we believe that the reality around us consists of
    what we learned to say it consists of._____

11. The principle of language use that explains the problem
    with a statement in a box that says, "All statements
    in this box are false."_____

12. The verb links two nouns, obscuring their differences at
    the silent and the verbal levels of abstraction and serves
    as a synonym for classification._____

13. The verb covers up the fact that impressions arise inside us
    so that we impute qualities to things._____

14. The process of examining reality—people and their actions,
    happenings, and objects—first ,and describing what
    occurred or what something looks like, second._____

15. Eliminating all forms of the verb To Be from our regular,
    everyday writing and conversations._____

16. The tendency to respond to events or people in terms of
    overgeneralized thinking._____

Instructions: Mark the following statements <u>C</u> for consistent with or <u>I</u> for inconsistent with the principles and philosophy discussed in this book. Do not consider the "truth" or "falsity" of the statement, only whether the statement appears consistent with the ideas or violates the ideas expressed in this book.

1. You can place your complete confidence in him since he has a long record of honorable dealings with others.   C I
2. A four-year old child told her mother that the red light means stop, the green light means go, and the yellow light means "go real fast."   C I
3. You can't trust George because he's a politician.   C I
4. Any person who hates children and dogs can't be all bad.   C I
5. Every American should feel proud when they see the flag go by.   C I
6. I've never settled for a grade below "A" and I don't intend to change my habits now.   C I
7. All people are created equal.   C I
8. My plans are to go to graduate school, get a master's degree, work a year, then get married and have three children.   C I
9. A philosopher was asked to make a statement that would apply to all situations; he replied: "And this too shall pass."   C I
10. He was very selfish and inconsiderate when I knew him in college, but I'm not sure what kind of person he is now.   C I
11. I was able to carry on with my work until I learned from my doctor that my illness was incurable.   C I
12. Set your goals and stick to them.   C I
13. Love me or leave me and let me be lonely; you won't believe me but I love you only. I'd rather be lonely than happy with somebody new.   C I
14. You can't teach an old dog new tricks.   C I
15. Give me that old-time religion; it was good enough for our fathers, so it is good enough for me.   C I
16. Every Near-Eastern Indian I've ever met has proved to be arrogant and overbearing in discussing international politics.   C I
17. Maybe some blondes have more fun, but bleaching your hair is no guarantee.   C I
18. You can never step in the same river twice.   C I
19. I confess that I enjoyed the bullfight, but don't make the mistake of thinking that I am that type of person.   C I
20 What's a nice girl like you doing in a place like this?   C I
21. I'm not going to get old fashioned about dress styles; I'm going to keep up with the latest fashions and buy cloth that's in style.   C I
22. You should honor your father and your mother, but don't believe everything they tell you.   C I
23. I've had a number of excellent meals in this restaurant, but you must judge for yourself.   C I
24. A skeptical adherent said to the Oracle: "Before I seek your advice, you must answer one question: Are you a true Oracle?"   C I

25. A play by Shakespeare is like a dress from Christian Dior;
     you know it will be good.   C I
26. Andy will not do very well in speech class because he has stage fright.   C I
27. You're never going to get me to wear a topless bathing suit,
     no matter how many others get them.   C I
28. I know I could never eat fried brains; I don't even like liver.   C I
29. The Bush Presidents are quite different from one another.   C I
30. Missy and I were to get married, until I found out that she had an affair with a
     traveling salesman when she was 16. I couldn't marry a girl like that.   C I

Unwarranted Inferences

Instructions: Read the following little story. Assume that all of the information has been reported accurately and represents a factual description. Read it carefully because some of the descriptions may lead you astray. You may refer back to the story whenever you wish.

Next, read the statements about the story and circle <u>T</u> to indicate that a statement rings definitely true for you; circle <u>F</u> to indicate that you think the statement sounds definitely false to you. Circle <u>U</u> to indicate that you don't feel certain about the statement; the statement doesn't sound true or false and you can't decide.

Answer each statement in turn, and do not go back to change any answer later and do not re-read any statements after you have answered them.

Story 1

You arrive home late one evening and you see the lights on in your living room. There is only one car parked in front of your house, and the words "Harold R. Jones, M.D." are spelled in small gold letters across one of the car's doors.

Statements about Story 1

1. The car parked in front of your house has lettering on one of its doors.   T F U
2. Someone in your family is sick.   T F U
3. No car is parked in front of your house.   T F U
4. The car parked in front of your house belongs to a man named Johnson.   T F U

Story 2

A Businessman had just turned off the lights in the store when a man appeared and demanded money. The owner opened a cash register. The contents of the cash register were scooped up, and the man sped away. A member of the police force was notified promptly.

Statements about Story 2

1. A man appeared after the owner had turned off his store lights.   T F U

2. The robber was a <u>man</u>.   T F U
3. The man who appeared did not demand money.   T F U
4. The man who opened the cash register was the owner.   T F U
5. The store owner scooped up the contents of the cash register and ran away.   T F U
6. Someone opened a cash register.   T F U
7. After the man who demanded the money scooped up the contents of the cash register, he ran away.   T F U
8. While the cash register contained money, the story does <u>not</u> state <u>how much</u>.   T F U
9. The robber demanded money of the owner.   T F U
10. A businessman had just turned off the light when a man appeared in the store.   T F U
11. It was broad daylight when the man appeared.   T F U
12. The man who appeared, opened the cash register.   T F U
13. No one demanded money.   T F U
14. The story concerns a series of events in which only three persons are referred to: the owner of the store, a man who demanded money, and a member of the police force.   T F U
15. The following events were included in the story: someone demanded money, a cash register was opened, its contents were scooped up, and a man dashed out of the store.   T F U

Symbol Usage

Instructions: Read the incidents carefully, then make your choice of answers quickly.

To make the longer stories easier to understand, part of some stories have been underlined. Your true or false response should relate specifically to the underlined part; if no part of the story is underlined, apply your answer to the entire story.

1. A Senator recently advised a group that, "In considering public issues it would be a good idea to find out what the Communists favor; if they take a unanimous stand for anything, it would be a pretty good rule to be against it." <u>You should consider this good advice.</u>   T F

2. If you were looking for a church to join and were invited to join a church that professed to be based on Communistic beliefs, would you (select one)
    a. refuse the invitation.
    b. report the group to a Senate investigating committee.
    c. determine what the church meant by the terms "Communist beliefs."

3. The constitution states that "All men are created equal." Scientific studies show "that children are born with great variations in mental and physical capacities." This discrepancy can be explained by realizing that **(select one)**

    a. the conflicting statements describe two different situations.

    b. our constitution is a very idealistic document.

    c. a constitution must only make general statements and not attempt to cover minor variations that exist in real life; otherwise it would become too large and unwieldy.

4. John bites into an apple and says, "This apple is sour." **Select one phrase** that indicates the "true" meaning of John's statement.

    a. This apple is low in sugar content.

    b. This apple is not ripe.

    c. This apple tastes sour to me.

5. Several ladies were asked to invite airmen to their homes for a New Year's Eve celebration. While standing outside the recreation hall of one of the squadrons, the ladies hear some swearing and some very dirty stories.

    These women all have children who will be in attendance at the parties.

    It would be **(select one)**

    a. Quite safe to invite these airmen to their celebrations.

    b. A good risk that the airmen would not act this way at the celebrations.

    c. Risky inviting these airmen to the celebrations where the airmen might also drink.

6. You discover that Mr. X is the only one of your hunting companions to receive the Distinguished Service Medal for bravery in the face of enemy fire. From this you have a logical right to decide **(select one)**

    a. that he would be an excellent person to take on the danger of our Tiger hunt.

    b. that any of your companions might be just as brave at tiger hunting asMr. X.

7. Mr. Y applies for a position as personnel director in your company. Years ago you remember Mr. Y was fairly evaluated as the most selfish, egotistical, narrow minded person in your high school class. To help you decide about hiring him, you should **(select one)**

    a. interview the people at his rooming house, the workers at his club, the barber who has been shaving him since he came to town three weeks ago and see what they say.

    b. check his letter of recommendation form the high school principal.

    c. check the caliber of the companies for which he worked before forming his own company 15 years ago.

8. If you desire to learn about a scientific or artistic activity, you should **(select one)**

    a. read all the fine materials published on the specific activity.

    b. hire an expert in the activity to tell you about it.

    c. experience the activity yourself.

9. One of the Scout laws states that "A Boy Scout is "clean." This means that Sam, an Eagle Scout (select one)
   a. maintains high standards of cleanliness in both mind and body.
   b. doesn't maintain high standards of cleanliness, but he has, as a scout, pledged himself to strive to maintain "clean" standards.

10. Because of a plane crash, you are forced to live with a family far back in the mountains. These people call their shoes "holy bibles." To effectively communicate with them, you should (select one)
   a. explain that it is sacrilegious to use the term "holy bibles" to refer to shoes.
   b. explain that the terms "Holy Bible" refers to the theology of Christianity.
   c. use the terms "holy bibles" to refer to shoes when talking with them.

Undifferentiated Judgments

Situation 1

Instructions: The following series of words are ones you see regularly in newspaper and magazines and hear and see on radio and television. Read the word, then, without hesitation, mark your reaction as to whether you feel the word pertains to "good" news or "bad" news. If it will help, think of the words as part of a newspaper headline.

Wall

Good _____ _____ _____ _____ _____ Bad

Compromise

Good _____ _____ _____ _____ _____ Bad

Probe

Good _____ _____ _____ _____ _____ Bad

Fixing

Good _____ _____ _____ _____ _____ Bad

Negotiate

Good _____ _____ _____ _____ _____ Bad

Situation 2

Instructions: Read each of the following words and then, immediately, place an "X" to indicate your perception of the word.

Bastard

Pleasant _____ _____ Unpleasant

Vomit

Pleasant _____ _____ Unpleasant

Love

Pleasant _____ _____ Unpleasant

Whore

Pleasant _____ _____ Unpleasant

Syphilis

Pleasant _____ _____ Unpleasant

Thinking Mode Profile

We measure Allness Thinking using the **Thinking Mode Inventory, a** unique instrument constructed for purposes of discovering the extent to which an individual leans toward optimistic versus pessimistic thinking. To complete the instrument, you should imagine that you did experience an unhappy event in your life and then write out a brief reason why you think the unhappy event occurred. After stating the reason why the unhappy event occurred, you analyze the reason you gave by providing an account of what happened. Then, you analyze the account by marking on a seven point scale (1) the extent to which the reason you gave had to do with you as a person, (2) the extent to which the unhappy event would occur in the future, and (3) the extent to which unhappy events might affect other aspects of your life.

Instructions: A brief description of three (3) unhappy events appears in the Inventory. Imagine that the event actually happened to you. Below the unhappy event write a reason why you think the unhappy event happened to you. Write your answer in the space provided.

For Example: Unhappy Event—You are late to an important party. You are devastated.

Reason—I was late for the party because I am always late; it runs in my family. I just can't help being late.

Note: The reason should be one that represents how you really feel. Just explain what you feel is an accurate reason.

Then, respond to the three questions listed below the reason. **These questions are about the reason which you wrote.** Circle the number (from 1 to 7) that represents the most accurate analysis of the reason.

For example, the above reason "I am always late; it runs in my family" might be scored a 2 for the first question because it has to do with you as a person, and it might be a 2 or 3 for the second question because it may cause you to miss future parties, and it might also be a 2 or 3 for the third question because it may also cause you to be late at school, at work, and for family gatherings.

Think about the reason you give for each incident and answer the three questions for each of them using your best judgment about why you chose that reason.

STATEMENT I: You miss an important party/social gathering. You are devastated.

Reason: I missed the party/social gathering because . . .

1. To what extent did the reason for missing the party/social gathering have to do with **you as a person,** your usual way of doing things, versus **something different than you as a person,** such as other people, circumstances, or luck?

The reason had to do with <u>me</u> as a person.   1 2 3 4 5 6 7

The reason had to do entirely with something other than me as a person.

2. To what extent was the reason something that caused you to miss only this party/social gathering versus causing you to miss parties/socials in the future?

The reason will cause me to miss future parties/socials   1 2 3 4 5 6 7

The reason me to miss only this party/social.

3. To what extent was the reason something that caused you to miss only this party/social gathering versus causing other unhappy events in your life?

The reason causes other unhappy events in my life.   1 2 3 4 5 6 7

The reason caused only this unhappy event in my life.

STATEMENT II. You are contradicted by a respected friend when you express an opinion. You are humiliated.

Reason: I was contradicted by my friend because . . .

4. To what extent did the reason for being contradicted have to do with **you as a person**, your usual way of doing things, versus **something different than you as a person,** such as other people, circumstances, or luck?

The reason had to do with <u>me</u> as a person.   1 2 3 4 5 6 7

The reason had to do entirely with something <u>other than</u> me as a person.

5. To what extent was the reason something that caused you to be contradicted at this particular time versus causing you to be contradicted in the future?

The reason will cause me to be contradicted in the future. 1 2 3 4 5 6 7

The reason caused me to be contradicted only this time.

6. To what extent was the reason something that caused you to be contradicted at this particular time versus causing other unhappy events in your life?

The reason causes other unhappy events in my life.   1 2 3 4 5 6 7

The reason caused only this unhappy event in my life.

STATEMENT III. You complete a project that contains errors. You are disappointed.
   Reason: I completed the project with several errors because . . .

7. To what extent did the reason for completing the project with several errors have to do with **you as a person**, your usual way of doing things, versus **something different than you as a person,** such as other people, circumstances, or luck?

The reason had to do with <u>me</u> as a person.	1 2 3 4 5 6 7	The reason had to do entirely with something <u>other than</u> me as a person.

8. To what extent was the reason something that caused you to complete the project with errors at this particular time versus causing you to complete projects with errors in the future?

The reason will cause me to complete a project with errors in the future.	1 2 3 4 5 6 7	The reason caused me to complete a project with errors only this time.

9. To what extent was the reason something that caused you to complete the project with errors at this particular time versus causing other unhappy events in your life?

The reason causes other unhappy events in my life.	1 2 3 4 5 6 7	The reason caused only this unhappy event in my life.

Part VI: Who?

Who Thought Up These Ideas?

Initial Thinker
Count Alfred Korzybski

Alfred was born 3 July 1879 and died 1 March 1950, during my freshman year at the University of Utah. He was the son of Ladislas, a Polish nobleman and a member of the imperial court, and Countess Helena Rzewuska Korzybski. His father worked as an engineer with the rank of General in the Ministry of Communication, a lover of mathematics and physics, but a pioneer in new methods of agriculture. Korzybie, the family estate and farm, was considered a model, to which the US Department of Agriculture sent representatives to study new methods, such as contour plowing and irrigation systems.

Alfred lived with his parents and an older sister in Warsaw, Poland. According to prevailing custom, the son of the gardener was chosen as his playmate. Later, with his father often at Court in St. Petersburg (now Leningrad) or traveling, young Alfred assumed the duties of supervising farming activities. The peasants loved the "little master" and he in turn looked after them, advised them, was their "doctor" when they needed medical help and none was available. While he was growing up, he learned to speak four languages, spending a half-day with a French governess, a half day with a German governess. Russian and Polish were taught in the schools. He learned English when he immigrated to America.

He was educated as a chemical engineer at the Polytechnic Institute in Warsaw and had interests in law, mathematics, and physics. At one time he taught mathematics, physics, French, and German at a gymnasium in Warsaw. He traveled as an eclectic scholar in Germany and Italy, he spent time in Rome and its university. He became friends with some Cardinals and others connected with the Vatican during the time of Pope Leo XIII.

When he returned from Rome, he was shocked to learn that his former playmate and all the other peasants could neither read nor write. Czarist law prohibited peasants from learning, keeping them illiterate. Nevertheless, he then built a small schoolhouse for the peasants on the country estate, for which he was sentenced to Siberia by the Russian government, but his father managed to have the sentence suspended.

At the outbreak of the First World War, he immediately volunteered for service in the Second Russian Army and was assigned to a special Cavalry Detachment of the General Staff Intelligence Department. In July he was ordered to the Ministry of War and sent to Petrograd, and by December of 1915 he was sent to Canada and the US as an artillery expert. He served in various capacities in the USA for the Russian Army until it collapsed, then he lectured for the US government to increase sales of war bonds. Later he became Secretary of the French-Polish Military Commission and Recruiting Officer for Ohio, Pennsylvania, and West Virginia.

In November 1918, he met Mira Edgerly, a native of Illinois and a portrait artist, noted for her work on ivory. They were married two months later in January 1919. Mira later explained that she had "never met anyone with such a capacity to care for humanity as a whole, as few men are capable of caring for one woman." One night he suddenly sat up in bed with tears dripping off his chin, and said to his wife, "Man is not an animal." He did not have the terms then, but to be free to work it out, he sought seclusion on his sister-in-law's Missouri farm, far from the interruptions of a demanding social life.

As one biographer wrote, "With his two fore-fingers bandaged after they had become inflamed and split with the typing, he picked out on an old "thrashing-machine" typewriter, the first draft of *Manhood of Humanity*. In that book he expounded and developed his new analytic functional definition of "man" as a "time-binding class of life". He took his crude manuscript, written in a language new to him, to the outstanding mathematical philosopher, Professor Cassius Jackson Keyser, Adrian Professor of Mathematics at Columbia University. Professor Keyser had been working on his own *Mathematical Philosophy* and had planned to finish it during his sabbatical year.

When he read the manuscript of Manhood of Humanity, he found that Korzybski had made a formulation that turned out to be the kernel he himself had been searching for all those years. Then, instead of completing his own book, he spent his time helping to edit Korzybski's manuscript, and made that new notion of man the thesis of his address to the Phi Beta Kappa Society in May 1921. Manhood of Humanity was published in early 1921.

While lecturing at the New School for Social Research in New York, Korzybski rapidly drew on the blackboard a diagram of the structural differential, which became a fundamental part of the presentation about the methods of General Semantics. In December of 1931, he delivered a paper before the American Mathematical Society on "A Non-Aristotelian System", then devoted his time during 1932 and 1933 to writing and editing. It wasn't until the book was already in type that he added the terms General Semantics to the title.

In June of 1938, the Institute of General Semantics was established and published the General Semantics Bulletin. In 1940 he became a naturalized citizen.

In 1942 a group of his students in Chicago, headed primarily by S.I. Hayakawa, founded the International Society for General Semantics. The Society published a new journal called ETC: A Review of General Semantics. He continued the work of the Institute, publishing 44 articles and his two books. He passed away on 1 March 1950.

Other Thinkers

J. Samuel Bois

J. Samuel Bois started his career in his native Quebec as a Catholic priest. As a worker-priest, he organized labor unions and founded a Catholic weekly which is still in existence. Then, as a missionary, he worked with Mexicans and Indians in California. But 14 years as a priest changed Sam Bois, and didn't change the church; he was arraigned and condemned before the Holy Office in Rome, subjected to what he calls "a latter-day Inquisition," and finally released from the church.

He returned to college, got a Ph.D. in psychology at McGill in Montreal, and joined with another psychologist in the first psychological consulting service in Canada. During that time he wrote a monthly column for a medical journal, a weekly column for a literary and political paper, and three books in French. During World War II, he served as a lieutenant colonel in charge of research and information at National Defense Headquarters in Ottawa.

In 1939 he "discovered" general semantics, and became a teacher of adult evening classes in general semantics in the San Francisco area; served as president of the San Francisco Chapter of the International Society for General Semantics (ISGS), and editor of The Map, the chapter's newsletter; and a member of the Editorial Committee of ETC., a journal of General Semantics. He went into industrial psychology after the Second World War and inserted many of his semantic ideas into that field.

Sam developed a management training program called Executive Methods which he conducted in many large cities. In 1956 he "retired" and moved to Southern California, where he served as director of research and education at Viewpoints Institute, a center for general semantics study in Los Angeles. He conducted classes and workshops there, at the University of California at Los Angeles, and at the University of Southern California. Some considered him the leading theoretician in general semantics at that time, as well as a valuable and exciting explorer of how to apply General Semantics in a person's life.

Bois--pronounced "bwa"—hasn't fallen into any simple category. He was neither an "orthodox Korzybskian" nor "merely a popularizer," whatever those terms meant. He built on Korzybski's foundations and developed insights that many found extremely useful. People in general semantics often have unusually diverse backgrounds, but few can match Sam Bois.

Jacob Brownowski

Jacob Bronowski was born in Łódź, Congress Poland, Russian Empire, in 1908. His family moved to Germany during the First World War, and then to England in 1920. Although, according to Bronowski, he knew only two English words on arriving in Great Britain, he gained admission to the Central Foundation Boys' School in London and went on to study at the University of Cambridge and graduated as the senior wrangler.

As a mathematics student at Jesus College, Cambridge, Bronowski co-edited—with William Empson—the literary periodical *Experiment*, which first appeared in 1928. Bronowski pursued this sort of dual activity, in both the mathematical and literary worlds, throughout his professional life. He was also a strong chess player, earning a half-blue while at Cambridge and composing numerous chess problems for the British Chess Magazine between 1926 and 1970.

He received a Ph.D. in mathematics in 1935, writing a dissertation in algebraic geometry. From 1934 to 1942 he taught mathematics at the University College of Hull. Beginning in this period, the British secret service MI5 kept Bronowski under surveillance, believing he was a security risk, which is thought to have restricted his access to senior posts in the UK.

During the Second World War Bronowski worked in operations research for the UK's Department of Home Security, where he developed mathematical approaches to bombing strategy for RAF Bomber Command. At the end of the war, Bronowski was part of a British team that visited Japan to document the effects of the atomic bombings of Hiroshima and Nagasaki. Subsequently, he became Director of Research for the National Coal Board in the UK.

In 1950, Bronowski wrote *The Common Sense of Science*, which, according to many, represents a splendidly and fresh analysis of the evolution of scientific thinking in a language common to all that is still as essential and topical today as when it was first published.

He first became familiar to the British public through appearances on the BBC television version of *The Brains Trust* in the late 1950s. His ability to answer questions on many varied subjects led to an offhand reference in an episode of *Monty Python's Flying Circus* where one character states that "He knows everything."

Following his experiences with the after-effects of the Nagasaki and Hiroshima bombings, he turned to biology, to better understand the nature of violence. Bronowski was an associate director of the Salk Institute in 1964.

In 1967 he delivered six Silliman Memorial Lectures at Yale University and chose as his subject the role of imagination and symbolic language in the progress of scientific knowledge. Transcripts of the lectures were published posthumously in 1978 as *The Origins of Knowledge and Imagination* and remain in print.

Bronowski is best remembered for his thirteen part series, *The Ascent of Man* (1973), a documentary about the history of human beings through scientific endeavor. During the making of *The Ascent of Man*, Bronowski was interviewed by the popular British chat show host Michael Parkinson, who later recounted that Bronowski's description of a visit to Auschwitz—Bronowski had lost many family members during the Nazi era—was one of Parkinson's most memorable interviews.

Jacob Bronowski married Rita Coblentz in 1941. The couple had four children, all daughters. He died in 1974 of a heart attack in East Hampton, New York a year after *The Ascent of Man* was completed, and was buried in the western side of London's Highgate Cemetery, near the entrance.

S.I. Hayakawa

Samuel Ichiye Hayakawa was born July 18, 1906 and died February 27, 1992. Of Japanese ancestry, he was a Canadian-born American academic and political figure. He served as an English professor, and as president of San Francisco State University and, then, from 1977 to 1983, as United States Senator from California. Born in Vancouver, British Columbia, Canada, he was educated in the public schools of Calgary, Alberta, and Winnipeg, Manitoba. He received an undergraduate degree from the University of Manitoba in 1927 and graduate degrees in English from McGill University in 1928 and the University of Wisconsin–Madison in 1935.

Hayakawa held the position of lecturer at the University of Chicago from 1950 to 1955. He served as a Professor of English at San Francisco State College (now called San Francisco State University) from 1955 to 1968. He became President of San Francisco State College during the turbulent period of 1968 to 1973, while Ronald Reagan served as governor of California, becoming president emeritus in 1973.

During 1968-69, a bitter strike occurred at the University for the purpose of establishing an Ethnic Studies program. It was a major news event and a chapter in the radical history of the United States and the Bay Area. The strike was led by the Third World Liberation Front, and supported by Students for a Democratic Society, the Black Panthers and the counter-cultural community, among others. It proposed 15 "non-negotiable demands," including a Black Studies department to be chaired by sociologist Nathan Hare and independent of the university administration; an open admission policy for all black students to "put an end to racism"; and an unconditional, immediate end to the War in Vietnam and the university's involvement with it.

Those in control of the strike threatened that if these demands were not immediately and completely satisfied, the entire campus was to be forcibly shut down. Hayakawa became popular with conservative voters in this period after he pulled the wires out from the loud speakers on a protesters' van at an outdoor rally, dramatically disrupting it. Hayakawa relented on December 6, 1968 and created the first-in-the-nation College of Ethnic Studies.

Hayakawa was elected to the United States Senate from California as a Republican in 1976, defeating incumbent Democrat John V. Tunney. Hayakawa served from January 3, 1977, to January 3, 1983. During a 1978 Senate debate over a pair of treaties to transfer possession of the Panama Canal and Canal Zone from the United States to Panama, Hayakawa said, "We should keep the Panama Canal. After all, we stole it fair and square." He did not run for reelection in 1982 and was succeeded by Republican Pete Wilson.

Hayakawa founded the political lobbying organization called "U.S. English," which sought to make the English language the official language of the United States. As a former U.S. senator in the late 1980s, he opposed the Civil Liberties Act of 1988, which provided for apologies and monetary reparations to persons of Japanese ancestry who were interned by the federal government during World War II.

Wendell Johnson

Wendell Johnson was an actor and author and a proponent of General Semantics. He was born in Roxbury, Kansas, April 16, 1906 and died in Iowa City, Iowa, August 29, 1965. The University of Iowa Hospitals and Clinics named The Wendell Johnson Speech and Hearing Center after him.

He married Edna Bockwoldt, May 31, 1929; children – Nicholas and Katherine. He served on the faculty of the University of Iowa from 1931 to 1965 as professor of Speech Pathology and Psychology; he became Director of the Speech Clinic in 1945. He was a member of the America Speech and Hearing Association (awarded honors in 1946 and was President in 1950); also President of the International Society for General Semantics; also member of the American Psychological Association, the Speech Association of America, and the American Association for the Advancement of Science.

Wendell Johnson is considered one of the earliest and most influential speech pathologists in the field; he spent most of his life trying to find the cause and cure for stuttering -- through teaching, research, scholarly and other writing, lecturing, supervision of graduate students, and persuading K-12 schools, the Veterans Administration, and other institutions of the need for speech pathologists. He played a major role in the creation of the American Speech and Hearing Association. Johnson's book *People in Quandaries: The Semantics of Personal Adjustment* (1946; still in print from the Institute of General Semantics) is an excellent introduction to general semantics applied to psychotherapy. *Your Most Enchanted Listener* was published in 1956; *Living With Change: The Semantics of Coping,* a collection of selected portions of transcriptions of hundreds of his talks, organized by Dorothy Moeller, and published posthumously in 1972, provided further general semantic insights. He also published many articles in his lifetime, in journals, including *ETC: A Review of General Semantics.* Neil Postman acknowledges the influence of *People in Quandaries* in his own excellent general semantics book, *Crazy Talk, Stupid Talk* (1976, Delacorte, New York).

Irving Lee

Irving Lee was born in New York on October 27, 1909. He attended New York University, where he majored in English and received his bachelor's degree in 1931. In 1932 he attended the Breadloaf School of English at Middlebury, Vermont. After three years of teaching the social sciences at Boonton (N.J.) High School, he went to Northwestern University as instructor in public speaking in the School of Speech. He received his M.A. degree at Northwestern in1935 and his Ph.D. in 1938. He became assistant professor in 1942, associate professor in 1947, and professor of public speaking in 1950. Irving J. Lee, professor in the School of Speech, Northwestern University, and long a leader in general semantics, passed away on May 23, 1955.

It was during his early years in Evanston that Dr. Lee first became interested in general semantics. In the autumn of 1939 he took his first intensive training seminar under Alfred Korzybski at the Institute of General Semantics, then in Chicago. He early became convinced of the value of general semantics in the improvement of public speaking, discussion, and debate, and in giving insight into the problems of communication which underlie human relations. In

February, 1940, under the direct influence of general semantics, he introduced his famous undergraduate course, "Language and Thought," which increased steadily in popularity, so that in recent years as many as 275 students have been enrolled in it at one time. In 1940 he also wrote his first book, *Language Habits in Human Affairs: An Introduction to General Semantics*, (1941) in which he undertook to explain in simple language the fundamental principles of general semantics, with an abundance of narrative and literary illustrations. Some consider this book the clearest and best introduction to Korzybski's basic ideas.

Elwood Murray

Elwood Murray was born in 1897 and raised on a farm near Hastings, Nebraska. He obtained a B.A. degree in 1922 from Hastings College, with majors in English and American History and received his M.A. in 1924 in Education and Speech at the University of Iowa, and a Ph.D. in Speech and Psychology from the University of Iowa in 1931. In 1931 Murray began teaching Speech at the University of Denver. From 1932 until his retirement in 1962, he directed the School of Speech at the University of Denver.

In 1949 he initiated the founding of the National Society for the Study of Communication, and served as its president in 1953. In the 1950s, he was among the first members of the Society for General Systems Research. He served as director of the Institute of General Semantics from 1967-1969; during his career, he served as chair, Interest Group in General Semantics and Related Methodologies, Speech Association of America; Board of Governors, International Society for General Semantics; Board of Trustees, Institute of General Semantics. He served as major professor on thirty-five doctoral dissertations. He authored *The Speech Personality* (Lippincott, 3rd Edition, 1956), *Integrative Speech,* with Barnard and Garland (Dryden, 1953), and the *Self-Perception Inventory for Speech*, with Miller (University of Denver, 1958).

He worked as the driving force in the development of the "communication process" as the unifying theory for the School of Speech at the University of Denver; he advocated the use of General Semantics as a key methodology in communication. In 1939 he participated in the first of five seminars with Alfred Korzybski in Chicago.He was married and with his wife, raised four children.

Anatol Rapaport

Rapoport was born in Lozovaya, Kharkov Governorate, Russia (in today's Kharkiv Oblast, Ukraine). In 1922, he came to the United States, and in 1928 he became a naturalized citizen. He started studying music in Chicago and continued with piano, conducting and composition at the Vienna Hochschule für Musik where he studied from 1929 to 1934. However, due to the rise of Nazism, he found it impossible to make a career as a pianist.

He shifted his career, receiving a Ph.D. degree in mathematics at the University of Chicago in 1941, enlisting in the U.S. Army Air Corps in 1941, serving in Alaska and India during World War II.[3]

After the war, he joined the Committee on Mathematical Biology at the University of Chicago (1947–1954), publishing his first book, *Science and the Goals of Man*, in 1950, co-authored with semanticist S. I. Hayakawa. He also received a one-year fellowship at the prestigious Center for Advanced Study in the Behavioral Sciences in Stanford, California. In 1954 Anatol Rapoport cofounded the Society for General Systems Research, along with the researchers Ludwig von Bertalanffy, Ralph Gerard, and Kenneth Boulding.

Rapoport was founding member, in 1955, of the Mental Health Research Institute (MHRI) at the University of Michigan. He became president of the Society for General Systems Research in 1965. In 1970 Rapoport moved to the University of Toronto as professor of mathematics and psychology (1970–79). He lived in bucolic Wychwood Park overlooking downtown Toronto, a neighbor of Marshall McLuhan. On his retirement from the University of Toronto, he became director of the Institute of Advanced Studies (Vienna) until 1983.

Anatol Rapoport died of pneumonia in Toronto. He was survived by his wife Gwen, daughter Anya, and sons Alexander and Anthony.

The Multitude of Un-Named Thinkers

Like the unobserved molecules, atoms, nuclei, and particles swirling in the universes of other levels of existence, we also acknowledge the vast array of unrecognized thinkers who wrestled with the concepts of reality, perceptions, and symbols. They made this treatise on the subject possible and our indebtedness reaches beyond even the least known phenomenon of our spiritual reality. We thank you.

What Others Wrote

Introduction

Bennis, Warren. 1966. Organizational Revitalization, *California Management Review*, Fall: 51-60.

Bourland, David D., Jr. 1966. The Semantics of a Non-Aristotelian Language, *Tenth International Conference on general Semantics, Denver, Co, August.*

Caplow, Theodore and McGee, Reece J. 1958. *The Academic Marketplace.* York: Basic Books.

Castro, Janice. 1989. Where did the gung-ho go? *Time*, September 11.

Johnson, Wendell. 1946. *People in Quandaries.* New York: Harper & Row, Publishers.

Professor X. 1973. *This Beats Working for a Living: The Dark Secrets of a College Professor.* New Rochelle, NY: Arlington House.

Riesman, David; Glazer, Nathan; and Denny, Reuel. 1953. *The Lonely Crowd,* New York: Doubleday Anchor Books.

Slater, Philip. 1970. *The Pursuit of Loneliness: American Culture at the Breaking Point.* Boston, MA: Beacon Press.

Stein, Jess (ed.). 1966. *The Random House Dictionary of the English Language.* York: Random House, Inc.

USA Today. 1991. Cover Story. September 23.

Zimbardo, Philip G. 1977. *Shyness: What it is, what to do about it?* Reading, MA: Addison-

Wesley Publishing Company.

Parts I, II, III, and IV

Aiken, Henry D (1956). *The Age of Ideology.* New York: Mentor Books, 1956.

Alexander, Hubert G (1967). *Language and Thinking.* Princeton, NJ: D. Van Nostrand Co, Inc.

Beardsley, Monroe C (1950). *Thinking Straight.* New York: Prentice-Hall, Inc., 1950.

Bois, J. Samuel (1978). *The Art of Awareness: a textbook on general semantics and epistemics.* Dubuque, Iowa, Wm. C. Brown Company Publishers.

Boulding, Kenneth (1956). *The Image.* Ann Arbor, MI: University of Michigan Press, 5-6.

Bronowski, Jacob (ca. 1950). *The Common Sense of Science.* New York: Vintage Press.

Burns, David D. (1980). *Feel Good: The New Mood Therapy.* New York: Signet Books, "Definitions of Cognitive Distortions," pp. 31-45.

Carroll, John B. (1956). *Language, Thought and Reality: Selected Writings of Benjamin Lee Whorf.* Cambridge, MA: The M.I.T. Press.

Chase, Stuart (1959). *Guides to Straight Thinking.* London: Phoenix House, 1959.

Gorman, Margaret (1962). *General Semantics and Contemporary Thomism.* Lincoln: University of Nebraska Press.

Haney, William V (1979). *Communication and Interpersonal Relations.* Homewood, Il.: Richard D. Irwin, Inc.

Harrison, Allen F. and Robert M. Bramson (1982). *The Art of Thinking.* New York: Berkley Books, 1982.

Hayakawa, S.I. (ed., 1962) *The Use and Misuse of Language.* New York: Harper & Brothers, Foreword, pp. vii-x.

Hodges, John C. and Mary E. Whitten (1977). *Harbrace College Handbook.* New York: Harcourt Brace Jovanovich, Inc.

Johnson, Wendell (1946). *People in Quandries: The Semantics of Personal Adjustment.* New York: Harper & Row, Publishers.

Kluger, Jeffrey (2013). The Discoverer, Fabiola Gianotti: Finding the Tiny Higgs Boson Took the Biggest Machine in the Arsenal of Physics—and Help from One Woman Obsessed with the Nature of Reality. *Time,* December 31, 2012-January 7, 2013, pp. 126, 128,130.

Korzybski, Count Alfred (1933, 1948). *Selections from Science and Sanity: An Introduction to Non-Aristotelian Systems and General Semantics.* Englewood, NJ: Institute of General Semantics.

Kushner, Harold S. (1981). *When Bad Things Happen to Good People.* New York: Avon.

Landau, L. D. and Rumer, G. B. (1960). *What is Relativity?* New York: Fawcett World Library.

Lee, Irving J. (1941). *Language Habits in Human Affairs.* New York: Harper & Brothers.

Martorano, Joseph T. and John P. Kildahl (1989). *Beyond Negative Thinking.* New York: Insight Books.

Morris, Charles (1938). Foundations of the Theory of Signs. *International Encyclopedia of Unified Science, Vol.* I, No. 2.

Murray, Elwood and Barbour, Alton (1973). Clinical General Semantics. *Journal of the American Society of Psychosomatic Dentistry and Medicine*, Vol. 20.

Murray, Elwood, Raymond H. Barnard, and J.V. Garland (1953). *Integrative Speech*. New York: The Dryden Press.

Pace, R. Wayne and Boren, Robert R. (1973). *The Human Transaction: Facets, Functions, and Forms of Interpersonal Communication*. Glenview, Illinois: Scott, Foresman and company, pp. 37-103.

Pace, R. Wayne (1992). When Bad Things Happen to Good Semanticists: New Thoughts on All-Inclusive Generalization, *ETC.: A Review of General Semantics*, Vol. 49, No. 1 (Spring), pp. 20-33.

Pace, R. Wayne, Peterson, Brent D. and Burnett, M. Dallas (1979). *Techniques for Effective Communication.* Reading, MA.: Addison-Wesley, 1979.

Rapoport, Anatol (1952). What is Semantics? *ETC: A Review of General Semantics*, Vol. 10, No. 1 (Autumn).

Rapoport, Anatol (1953). *Operational Philosophy: Integrating Knowledge and Action*. New York: Harper & Row, Inc.

Rapoport, Anatol (1962). Introduction: What is Semantics? In S.I. Hayakawa (ed.) The Use and Misuse of Language. New York: Harper & Brothers, pp. 11-25.

Schlauch, Margaret (1955). *The Gift of Language*. New York: Dover Publications.

Searle, John R. The Construction of Social Reality. New York: The Free Press, 1995.

Seligman, Martin E.P. and Peter Schulman (1986). "Explanatory Style as a Predictor of Productivity and Quitting Among Life Insurance Sales Agents," *Journal of Personality and Social Psychology*, 50, pp. 832-838.

Selltiz, Claire; Johoda, Marie; Deutsch, Morton; and Cook, Stuart W. (1964). *Research Methods in Social Relations*. New York: Holt, Rinehart and Winston.

Smith, Donald G. (1976). *How to Cure Yourself of Positive Thinking*. Miami, Fl: E.A. Seemann Publishing, Inc.

Snider, James G. (1969). Studies of All-inclusive Conceptualization, *General Semantics Bulletin,* Vol. 36, pp. 51-54.

Trotter, Robert J. (1987). "Stop Blaming Yourself," *Psychology Today,* February, 31-39.

Weaver, Carl H. and Strausbaugh, Warren L. (1964). *Fundamentals of Speech Communication*. New York: American Book Company.

The Author

R. Wayne Pace

Dr. Pace is Professor Emeritus of Organizational Leadership, Marriot School of Management, Brigham Young University, a Professor of Communication, and an independent consultant and management development specialist. His research specialties include Modes of Thinking and Operating Styles and Work Perceptions. He is the author of approximately thirty (30) books and more than one hundred (100) technical and popular articles. He taught General Semantics at three different universities, including an Honors Course and published "When Bad Things Happen to Good Semanticists" in *ETC,* a journal about General Semantics, reporting research on the concept of "allness" and its dimensions. He served as president of the International Communication Association, the Western States Communication Association, and the Academy of Human Resource Development.

Appendix A

Pre-Reading Assessment Answers

1. F 26. F
2. F 27. T
3. F 28. F
4. F 29. F
5. F 30. F
6. F 31. T
7. T 32. F
8. F 33. F
9. F 34. F
10. F 35. T
11. F 36. T
12. F 37. T
13. F 38. F
14. F 39. F
15. T 40. F
16. F 41. T
17. T 42. T
18. F 43. T
19. F 44. T
20. T 45. T
21. F 46. T
22. T 47. T
23. F 48. F
24. F 49. F
25. F 50. T

Appendix B

Answers to Post-Reading Assessment by Category

Meaning of Concepts

    1. The ancient, classical, Aristotelian view of people and reality

    2. Cause-effect, Newtonian view of people and reality

    3. Modern, scientific, probabilistic, Einsteinian view of people and reality

Names of Concepts

    4. Truth

    5. Science

    6. Relativity

    7. Abstracting

    8. Multiordinality

    9. First-Order Experience

    10. Circularity

    11. Self-reflexiveness

    12. Identify

    13. Predication or Projection

    14. Extensional Orientation

    15. E-Prime English

    16. Allness

Statements Consistent with Contemporary Theory

1.	I
2.	C
3.	I
4.	C
5.	I
6.	I
7.	I
8.	I
9.	C
10.	C
11.	I
12.	I
13.	I
14.	I

15.	I
16.	C
17.	C
18.	C
19.	I
20.	I
21.	I
22.	C
23.	C
24.	I
25.	I
26.	I
27.	I
28.	I
29.	C
30.	I

Unwarranted Inferences
Story 1

1.	T
2.	F
3.	?
4.	?

Story 2

1.	?
2.	?
3.	F
4.	?
5.	?
6.	T
7.	?
8.	?
9.	?
10.	?
11.	T
12.	?
13.	?
14.	T
15.	T

16.	?
17.	?
18.	?

Symbol Usage

1.	F	Bi-Polarism
2.	C	Signal Reaction
3.	A	One Meaning Fallacy
4.	C	Projection
5.	B	Where Index
6.	B	Where Index
7.	A	When Index
8.	C	Extensional Orientation
9.	B	Predication
10.	C	Naming Classifications

Undifferentiated Judgments

We know that reality has greater differentiations than language, so when we use language to talk about differences among people, objects, or happenings, we have a tendency to provide for only two or possibly three alternatives. Thus, our language, as used in everyday interpersonal interaction tends toward bipolar choices. Polarization consists of talking about a person, thing, or event by placing our perceptions and evaluations on one end of a two-pole choice that appears to represent dichotomous or mutually exclusive choices. Polarization encourages the inclination of people to create either-or categories and ignore or eliminate any gradations. Polarization occurs when we treat contrary or scaled reactions as contradictory or truly either-or situations.

Situation 1 allows you to judge a contrary situation in terms of a contradictory good-bad bipolar set. If you placed an X at either end of the bipolar choices, you tend to violate the principle of contrary judgments.

Situation 2 allows you to judge your reactions to potentially Taboo Words. If you have a tendency to select the bipolar end, you tend to violate the principle of contrary judgments.

Thinking Mode Profile

Scores and Interpretations

Scoring: Derive your scores on the Thinking Mode Profile by summing the items reflecting each of the primary variables of Source, Time, and Space as indicated in the Scoring Key. Derive the average score for each variable across all three incidents by summing the scores and dividing by three. Sum the averages for each of the three primary variables and divide by three to determine the TM Index Score. The Index Score should be expressed as a figure ranging from 1.0 to 7.0.

Source	Time	Space	
Incident I.	Missed	Social Gathering	
1 _____	2. _____	3. ____	I Total ____
Incident II. Contradicted by Friend			
4 ____	5 ____	6 ____	II Total ____
Incident III. Project Completed with Errors			
7 _____	8 _____	9 _____	III Total _____

Interpretation of Scores: Your TM Index score may be interpreted in the following way:

If your index score is 5.51 or higher, you have a very positive way of reacting to unhappy events in your life.

If your index score is between 4.01 and 5.50, you tend to react to unhappy events in your life slightly positively or slightly negatively, depending on your mood for the day.

If your index score is 4.0 or lower, you have a somewhat negative way of reacting to unhappy events in your life.

Those who react negatively to unhappy events feel that they are the cause of unhappiness in their lives, and that unhappiness is with them all the time and everywhere. Persistent negative reactions or pessimism lead to feelings of hopelessness and helplessness in coping with life.

Those who react positively to unhappy events feel that the cause of unhappiness in their lives is something other than them personally, and that unhappiness occurs only occasionally and in limited situations. An optimistic view of life comes from reacting to negative events in a positive way.

Answers to Post-Reading Assessment by Number

1. F	26. F	49. T	74. 7
2. F	27. F	50. F	75. 4
3. F	28. T	51. B	76. 8
4. F	29. F	52. E	77. 11
5. T	30. T	53. G	78. 5
6. F	31. T	54. I	79. C
7. T	32. T	55. J	80. A
8. F	33. F	56. H	81. B
9. T	34. T	57. F	
10. T	35. F	58. D	
11. T	36. F	59. A	

12. F	37. F	60. C
13. F	38. T	61. C
14. F	39. T	62. C
15. T	40. T	63. D
16. F	41. F	64. C
17. T	42. T	65. D
18. T	43. T	66. 9
19. F	44. F	67. 6
20. F	45. T	68. 2
21. F	46. T	69. 10
22. T	47. F	70. 13
23. T	48. F	71. 1
24. F		72. 12
25. T		73. 3

Index